August 1, 1991

Happy 6th Birthday
    Kyle!

  lots of love,
  Judy, Chic, and Rick

FIRST PICTURE
ATLAS

Photographic Acknowledgements

The publishers would like to thank the following for their
kind permission to reproduce the following photographs:

Eurotunnel 37;
Susan Griggs Agency/Alastair Scott 26, Charles W Friend
47 right, Ian Murphy 62;
Robert Harding Picture Library 3 right, 23, 28, 36, 41, 43,
47 left, 56;
Hutchison Library Front cover, 19, 24, 51, 61;
Frank Lane Picture Agency/S McCutcheon 8;
James Milne, Back cover
Popperfoto 32
Frank Spooner Pictures 49
Tony Stone Associates 1, 3 left and centre, 21, 39, 45, 53,
54;
Zefa Picture Library 31, 58

Photographs

Front cover: New York City
Back cover: The Nile, Egypt
Page 1: Fishing boats in Norway
Page 3 (from left to right): Bali dancers; A view of Ginza, Tokyo, Japan;
A view of Accademia Bridge, Venice.

This book first published in 1989 by Gallery Books
An imprint of W. H. Smith Publishers Inc.
112 Madison Avenue
New York City 10016

By arrangement with Octopus Books Limited

© Copyright Octopus Books Limited 1989

ISBN 0 8317 3361 6

Printed in Hungary

FIRST PICTURE
ATLAS

GALLERY BOOKS
An Imprint of W. H. Smith Publishers Inc.
112 Madison Avenue
New York City 10016

MAP OF MAPS

This is a very special map. It tells you on which pages of the atlas you will find the chief maps of all the countries. If you want to find the chief map of the USSR, look right across the Map of Maps until you find the name USSR. This is called scanning the map. When you find it, you will see that the chief map of USSR is on pages 46 and 47. Now scan the Map of Maps for the USA.

There are lots of small countries in Europe. They are all crowded together and cannot be shown clearly on the big Map of Maps. They have therefore been put on a small extra map. This is called an inset map. An inset map shows things and places which are too small to show on the main map.

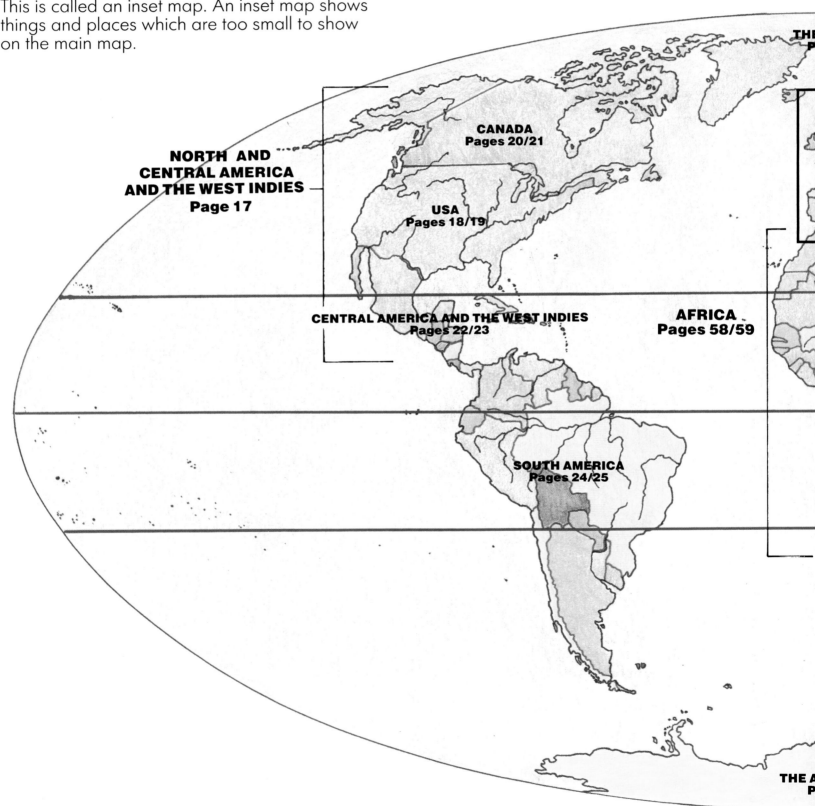

CANADA
Pages 20/21

NORTH AND
CENTRAL AMERICA
AND THE WEST INDIES
Page 17

USA
Pages 18/19

CENTRAL AMERICA AND THE WEST INDIES
Pages 22/23

AFRICA
Pages 58/59

SOUTH AMERICA
Pages 24/25

THE
P.

THE A
P.

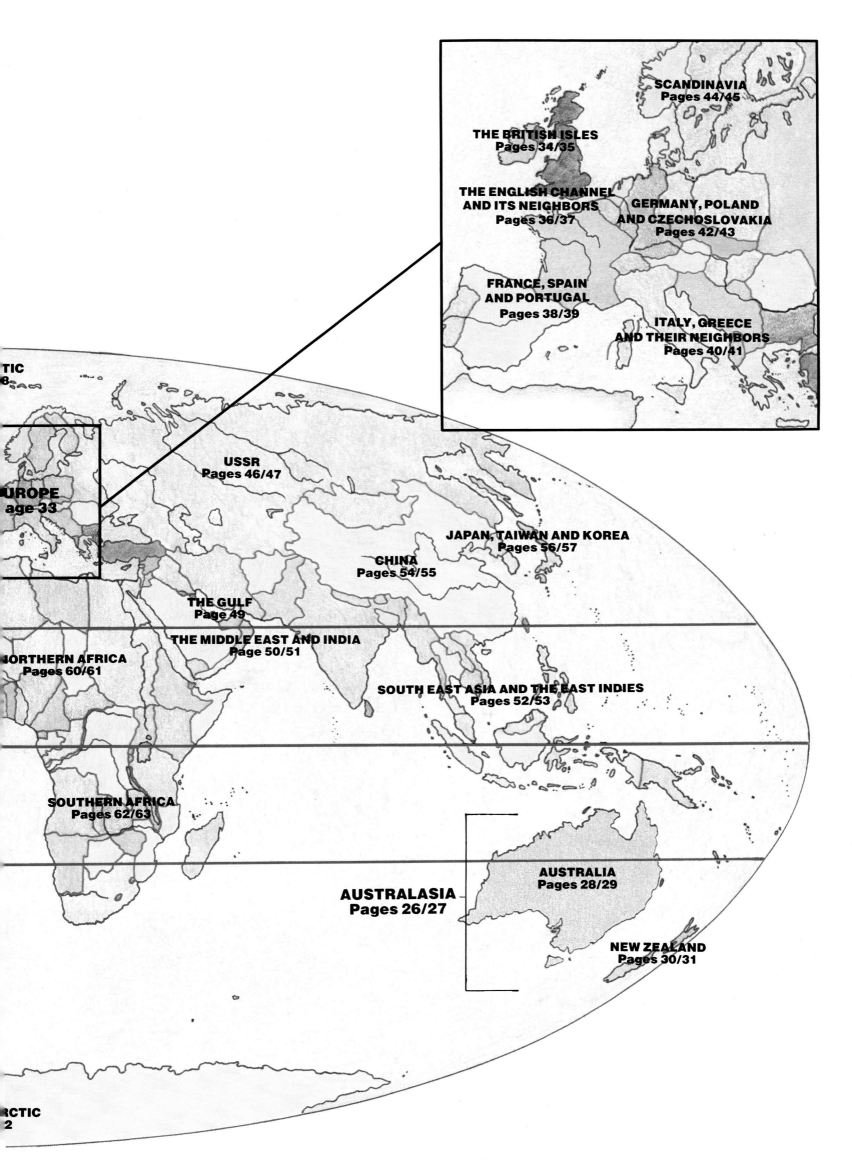

SCANDINAVIA
Pages 44/45

THE BRITISH ISLES
Pages 34/35

THE ENGLISH CHANNEL
AND ITS NEIGHBORS
Pages 36/37

GERMANY, POLAND
AND CZECHOSLOVAKIA
Pages 42/43

FRANCE, SPAIN
AND PORTUGAL
Pages 38/39

ITALY, GREECE
AND THEIR NEIGHBORS
Pages 40/41

TIC
8

UROPE
age 33

USSR
Pages 46/47

JAPAN, TAIWAN AND KOREA
Pages 56/57

CHINA
Pages 54/55

THE GULF
Page 49

THE MIDDLE EAST AND INDIA
Page 50/51

NORTHERN AFRICA
Pages 60/61

SOUTH EAST ASIA AND THE EAST INDIES
Pages 52/53

SOUTHERN AFRICA
Pages 62/63

AUSTRALIA
Pages 28/29

AUSTRALASIA
Pages 26/27

NEW ZEALAND
Pages 30/31

RCTIC
2

OUR EARTH
IN SPACE

Our Earth seems very big to us, but it is really very small. The Earth is one of nine planets going round our Sun once every year. Other planets go round our Sun too. Some, like Mercury, are hotter than Earth. Some planets, like Neptune, are colder than Earth. Most planets are bigger than Earth, but some are smaller. Look at the inset picture to see which is the biggest planet of all.

The Sun is really just a star, like all the other stars in the sky. But it looks big and round and orange because it is nearer to us than the others.

Just as the Earth goes round the Sun, so our Moon goes round the Earth. This takes four weeks, almost a month on the calendar. We say that the Moon is a satellite of the Earth, and we say that the Earth is a satellite of the Sun.

The Sun and all the planets together are called the Solar System. The Solar System is only a tiny part of a great galaxy called The Milky Way. This is made up of countless millions and millions of stars and their satellites.

The Milky Way is our own galaxy. But there are millions of others. They are so far away that they look just like stars themselves.

We use telescopes to see these things. But we can also send people up into Space. They are called astronauts. Sometimes we send up cameras and other instruments. Some of these go round and round the Earth, taking pictures. They are called satellites too. The pictures they take help us to make our maps correct. Some of the instruments are just sent on and on into Space. These are called space probes, and they send us messages about planets we can never land on.

Inset right: The planets in our Solar System

2	Mercury	5	Mars	8	Uranus
3	Venus	6	Jupiter	9	Neptune
4	Earth	7	Saturn	10	Pluto

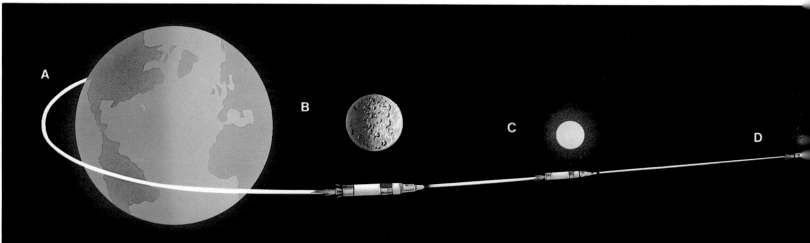

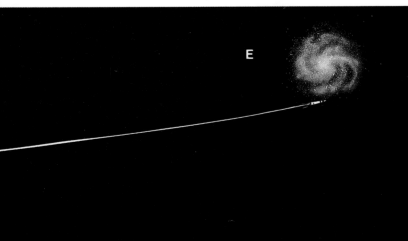

Above: The Solar System. 1 Sun   2 Mercury   3 Venus
4 Earth   5 Mars   6 Jupiter   7 Saturn   8 **Uranus**
9 Neptune   10 Pluto

Left: How big is space? Space is a huge area beyond the
atmosphere of the Earth. This diagram tries to show how great the
distance in space is by showing the time it would take a space
rocket to travel into space if it was traveling at 17,400 miles per hour.

A The Earth
B The Moon: 2½ days
C The Sun: 3 weeks
D The nearest star: 500,000 years
E The nearest galaxy: 20,000 million years

OUR RESTLESS EARTH

Our Earth has a crust, or skin, which is quite cool, thin and solid. Most of it is covered by the waters of the oceans. We live only on the lands which rise up between the oceans. These are the continents, such as North America and Asia. The crust is cracked into a few large pieces. We call these plates. Some of the cracks are under the oceans; others run across the continents.

Underneath the Earth's crust it is so hot that the rock is almost liquid. It is hot enough to melt, but the pressure of the crust keeps it in place, so it is more like syrup. This syrupy rock is called magma. The plates of the crust lie on top of the

Above right: Damage caused by an earthquake in Alaska in 1964. Sometimes the crust of the Earth cracks. If this happens suddenly, the ground shakes. This is called an earthquake; buildings fall down and people may be killed.

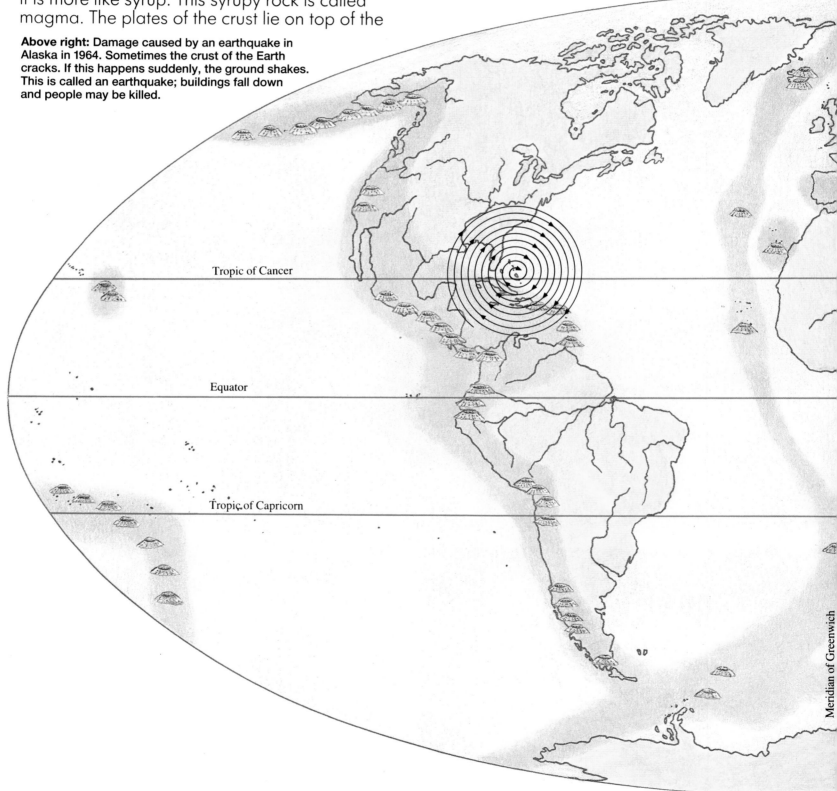

Tropic of Cancer

Equator

Tropic of Capricorn

Meridian of Greenwich

8

Areas of hurricanes, cyclones and typhoons	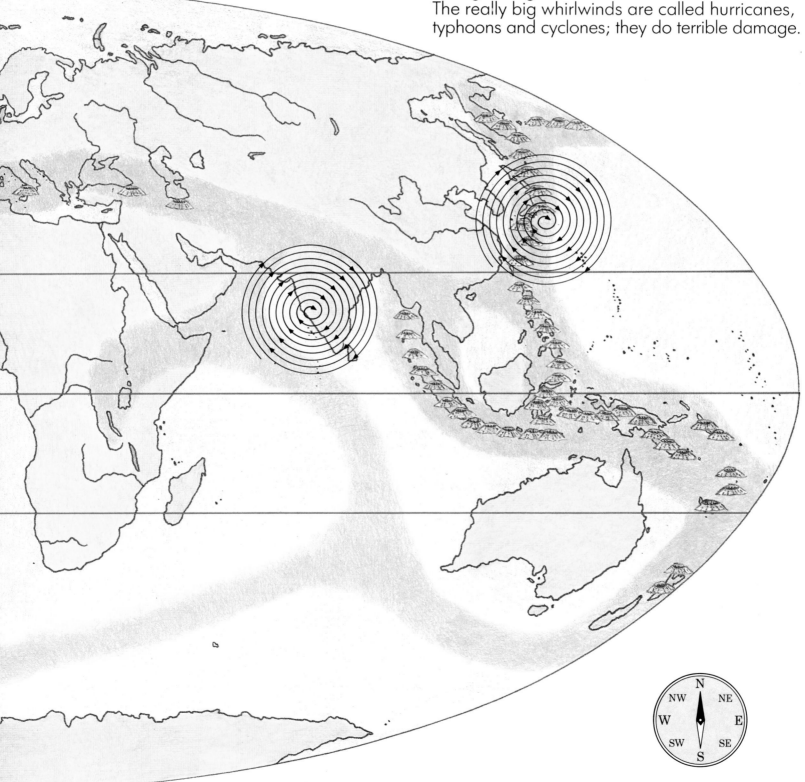
Area of earthquakes	
Volcanoes	

magma, like rafts floating on syrup. The magma moves very slowly and it carries the plates along with it.

Sometimes these plates crash into one another. When they collide, their edges crack and crumple, and form great mountain ranges. When the ground cracks, we feel it as an earthquake. Houses may be shaken down, and dams might break, causing floods. Sometimes we see volcanoes. This is when the magma escapes through a gap between the plates and turns into lava. People may be choked by dust and by poisonous gas.

A thin film of air goes all round our Earth. This air is always moving about, sometimes bringing rain, sometimes drought. Sometimes the air spins round and round, faster and faster, until it is strong enough to blow off the roof of a house. The really big whirlwinds are called hurricanes, typhoons and cyclones; they do terrible damage.

HOW TO DECODE THE MAPS

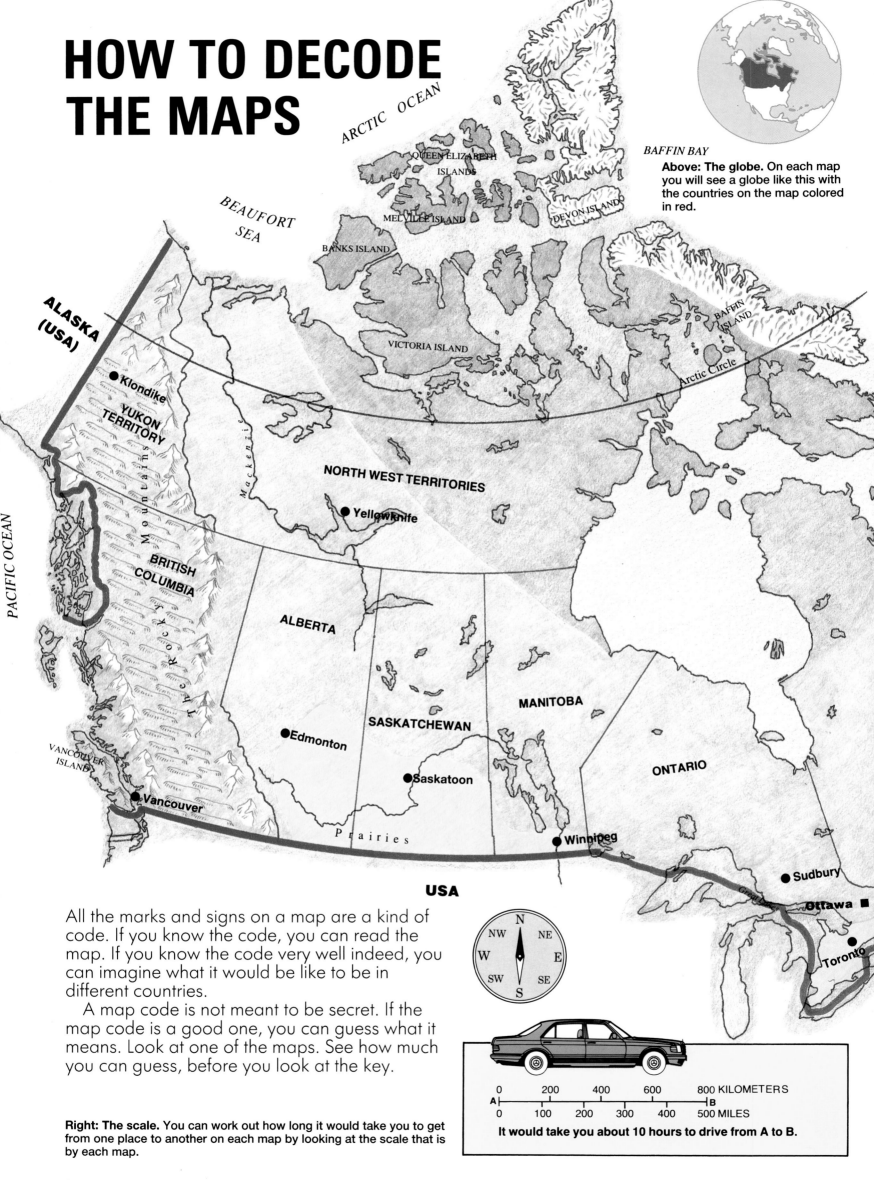

ARCTIC OCEAN

QUEEN ELIZABETH ISLANDS

BAFFIN BAY

Above: The globe. On each map you will see a globe like this with the countries on the map colored in red.

BEAUFORT SEA

MELVILLE ISLAND

DEVON ISLAND

BANKS ISLAND

BAFFIN ISLAND

ALASKA (USA)

• Klondike

YUKON TERRITORY

VICTORIA ISLAND

Arctic Circle

PACIFIC OCEAN

Mackenzie

NORTH WEST TERRITORIES

• Yellowknife

Mountains

BRITISH COLUMBIA

The Rockies

ALBERTA

VANCOUVER ISLAND

•Edmonton

SASKATCHEWAN

MANITOBA

ONTARIO

•Saskatoon

•Vancouver

Prairies

•Winnipeg

• Sudbury

USA

Ottawa ■

Toronto

Great Lakes

All the marks and signs on a map are a kind of code. If you know the code, you can read the map. If you know the code very well indeed, you can imagine what it would be like to be in different countries.

A map code is not meant to be secret. If the map code is a good one, you can guess what it means. Look at one of the maps. See how much you can guess, before you look at the key.

Right: The scale. You can work out how long it would take you to get from one place to another on each map by looking at the scale that is by each map.

N
NW   NE
W   E
SW   SE
S

0	200	400	600	800 KILOMETERS

A   B

0	100	200	300	400	500 MILES

It would take you about 10 hours to drive from A to B.

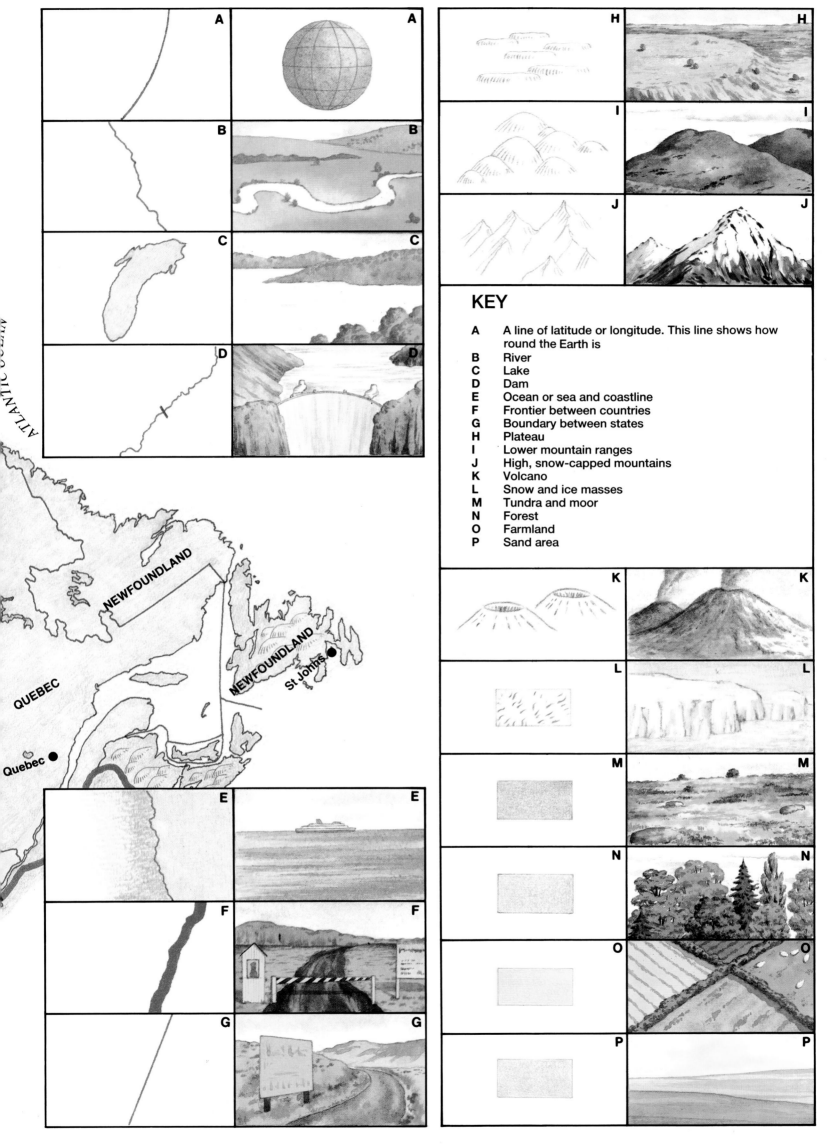

KEY

A   A line of latitude or longitude. This line shows how round the Earth is
B   River
C   Lake
D   Dam
E   Ocean or sea and coastline
F   Frontier between countries
G   Boundary between states
H   Plateau
I   Lower mountain ranges
J   High, snow-capped mountains
K   Volcano
L   Snow and ice masses
M   Tundra and moor
N   Forest
O   Farmland
P   Sand area

HOW MAPS ARE MADE

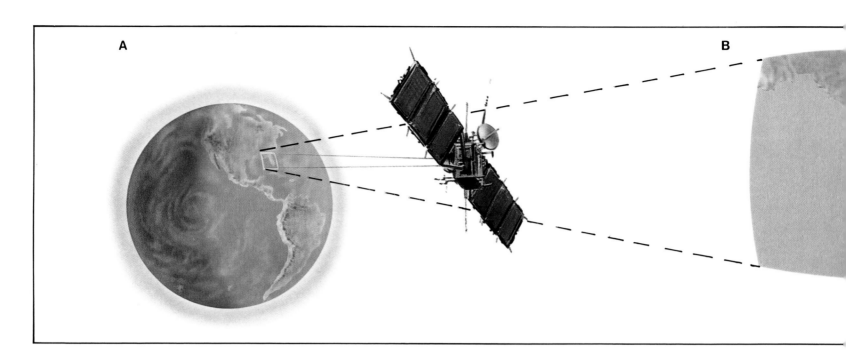

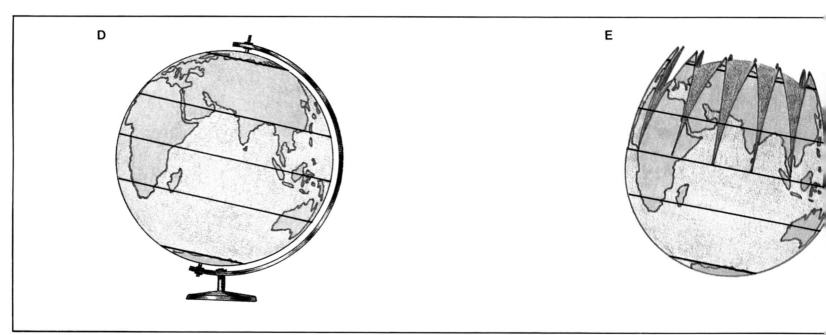

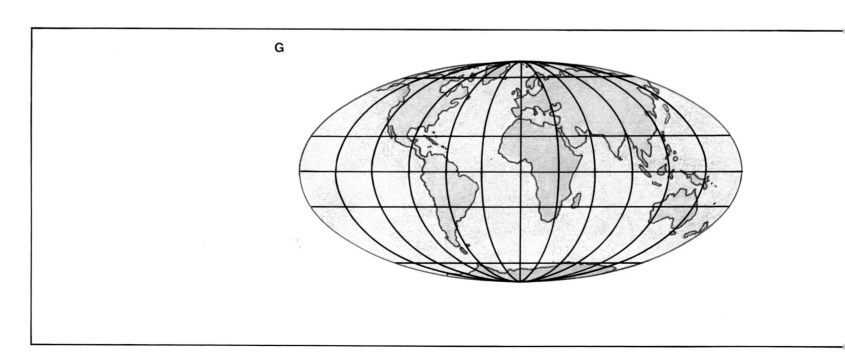

C

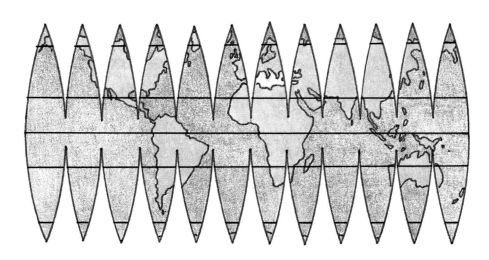

F

A   A satellite takes a picture of a part of the Earth (eg Florida).
B   The picture of Florida.
C   A map is drawn from this picture.
D   Lots of maps are put together to make a globe of the world.
E   If we peel the map off a globe it is still curved.
F   If we press the map flat, it is still split. So we must stretch and bend the points together to make a picture of the whole world (G).

COUNTRIES OF THE WORLD

A country is a piece of land where the people have their own king, or president or other ruler. Sometimes a country was formed because all the people spoke the same language, like the people of France. Sometimes the people had the same religion and prayed together like the Moslems of Pakistan. Sometimes they had their own history and way of life, like the Chinese.

There are always some countries, somewhere, quarreling and fighting. Almost all countries are now members of the United Nations. They meet regularly and this gives them a chance to talk instead of fight.

34	KUWAIT
35	BAHRAIN
36	UNITED ARAB EMIRATES
37	OMAN
38	SOUTH YEMEN
39	YEMEN
40	IRAN
41	AFGHANISTAN
42	PAKISTAN
43	INDIA
44	NEPAL
45	BANGLADESH
46	BHUTAN
47	CHINA
48	USSR
49	NORTH KOREA
50	SOUTH KOREA
51	JAPAN
52	TAIWAN
53	HONG KONG
54	VIETNAM
55	LAOS
56	BURMA
57	THAILAND
58	KAMPUCHEA
59	SRI LANKA

62	INDONESIA
63	PAPUA NEW GUINEA
64	SOLOMON ISLANDS
65	VANUATA
66	FIJI
67	NEW CALEDONIA
68	CHATAM ISLANDS
69	NEW ZEALAND
70	AUSTRALIA
71	ANTARCTICA
72	SOUTH AFRICA
73	LESOTHO
74	SWAZILAND
75	MADAGASCAR
76	MOZAMBIQUE
77	ZIMBABWE
78	BOTSWANA
79	NAMIBIA
80	ANGOLA
81	ZAMBIA
82	MALAWI
83	TANZANIA
84	BURUNDI
85	RWANDA

1	UNITED KINGDOM
2	REPUBLIC OF IRELAND
3	NORWAY
4	SWEDEN
5	FINLAND
6	DENMARK
7	NETHERLANDS
8	BELGIUM
9	FRANCE
10	SPAIN
11	PORTUGAL

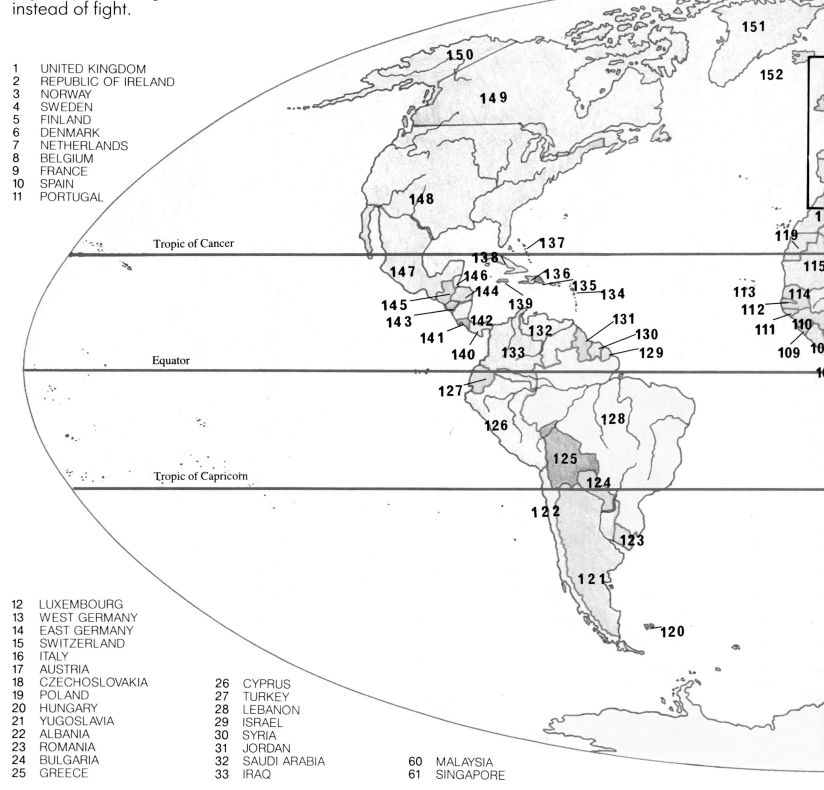

12	LUXEMBOURG
13	WEST GERMANY
14	EAST GERMANY
15	SWITZERLAND
16	ITALY
17	AUSTRIA
18	CZECHOSLOVAKIA
19	POLAND
20	HUNGARY
21	YUGOSLAVIA
22	ALBANIA
23	ROMANIA
24	BULGARIA
25	GREECE

26	CYPRUS
27	TURKEY
28	LEBANON
29	ISRAEL
30	SYRIA
31	JORDAN
32	SAUDI ARABIA
33	IRAQ

60	MALAYSIA
61	SINGAPORE

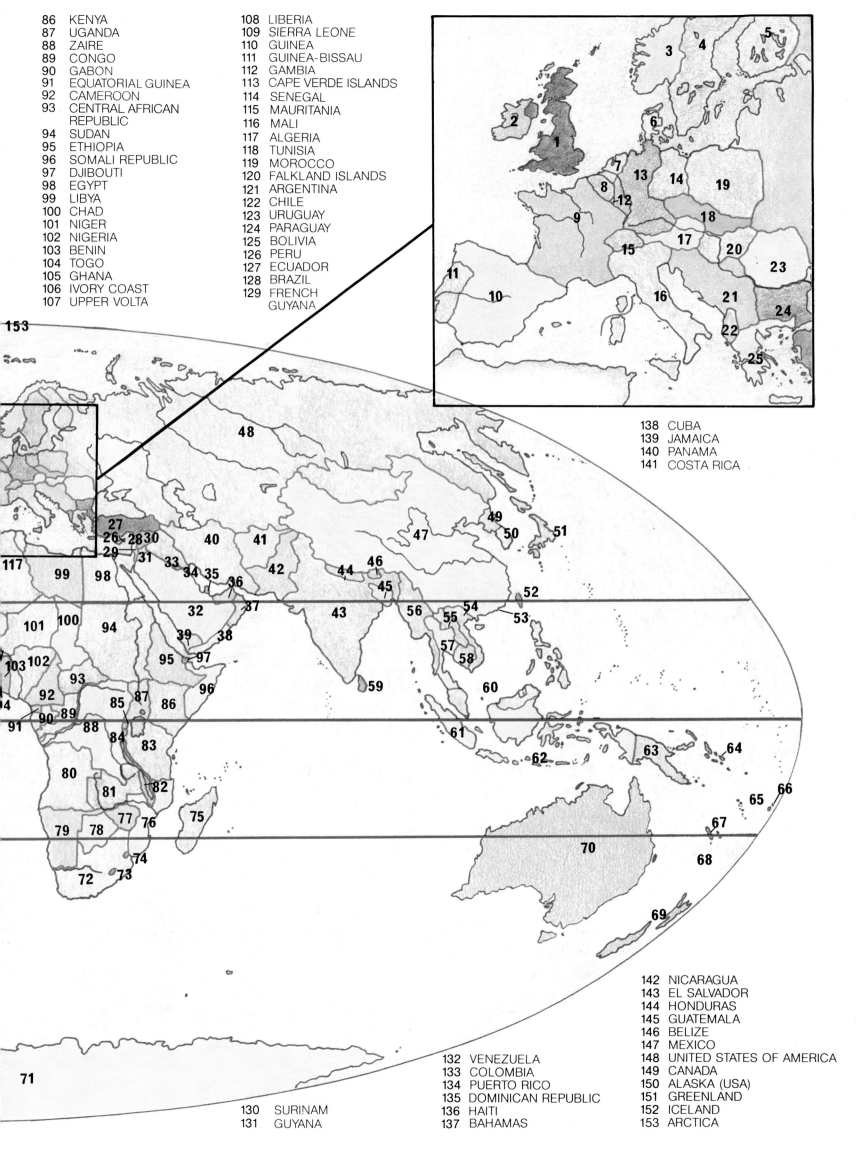

86 KENYA
87 UGANDA
88 ZAIRE
89 CONGO
90 GABON
91 EQUATORIAL GUINEA
92 CAMEROON
93 CENTRAL AFRICAN
   REPUBLIC
94 SUDAN
95 ETHIOPIA
96 SOMALI REPUBLIC
97 DJIBOUTI
98 EGYPT
99 LIBYA
100 CHAD
101 NIGER
102 NIGERIA
103 BENIN
104 TOGO
105 GHANA
106 IVORY COAST
107 UPPER VOLTA

108 LIBERIA
109 SIERRA LEONE
110 GUINEA
111 GUINEA-BISSAU
112 GAMBIA
113 CAPE VERDE ISLANDS
114 SENEGAL
115 MAURITANIA
116 MALI
117 ALGERIA
118 TUNISIA
119 MOROCCO
120 FALKLAND ISLANDS
121 ARGENTINA
122 CHILE
123 URUGUAY
124 PARAGUAY
125 BOLIVIA
126 PERU
127 ECUADOR
128 BRAZIL
129 FRENCH
    GUYANA

138 CUBA
139 JAMAICA
140 PANAMA
141 COSTA RICA

142 NICARAGUA
143 EL SALVADOR
144 HONDURAS
145 GUATEMALA
146 BELIZE
147 MEXICO
148 UNITED STATES OF AMERICA
149 CANADA
150 ALASKA (USA)
151 GREENLAND
152 ICELAND
153 ARCTICA

132 VENEZUELA
133 COLOMBIA
134 PUERTO RICO
135 DOMINICAN REPUBLIC
136 HAITI
137 BAHAMAS

130 SURINAM
131 GUYANA

SYMBOLS USED IN THIS BOOK

There are pictures, or symbols, on all the maps in this book. They will tell you more about the places you are looking at. Here are some of the pictures you will find. Some pictures will tell you about farming. Other pictures will tell you about what kind of work people do, such as mining or shipbuilding. You can look back to this page as you study each map.

Apples		Caviar		Wheat		Oil	
Coconuts		Cocoa		Whisky		Offshore oil	
Lemons		Dates		Wine		Oil pipeline	
Oranges		Maize		Olives		Rubber	
Pineapples		Palm oil		Coffee		Ship building	
Beef cattle		Peanuts		Sunflowers		Timber	
Dairy cattle		Rice		Coal mining		Silk	
Fish		Soya beans		Mining		Cotton	
Pigs		Sugar cane		Diamond mining		Capital city e.g. ■ London	
Sheep		Tea		Factories		City e.g. ● New York	
Whales		Tobacco		Electricity		Mountain e.g. ▲ Mount Everest	

NORTH AND CENTRAL AMERICA WITH THE WEST INDIES

Many countries have a share of this large continent. The United States of America (USA) is one of the biggest and has most of the good land and good weather. It is made up of 50 different areas called states. It is so well known that we often call it the United States (US) or just America. The capital city of the USA is Washington. Washington is not in any of the states. It has a piece of land all to itself, called the District of Columbia.

The capital of Canada is Ottawa. Canada stretches almost to the North Pole. To the east of Canada is Greenland. Greenland is a large island which belongs to Denmark. Next to Greenland is another island: Iceland.

In the far south, the continent gets very narrow. This bit is called Central America. Mexico has the widest part, but the narrow part is shared by many small countries. Can you see all the names?

In the sea there are thousands of islands. Some of them are separate countries. Cuba and Jamaica are like this. But some of the very small islands still belong to Britain, France or Holland who captured them long ago.

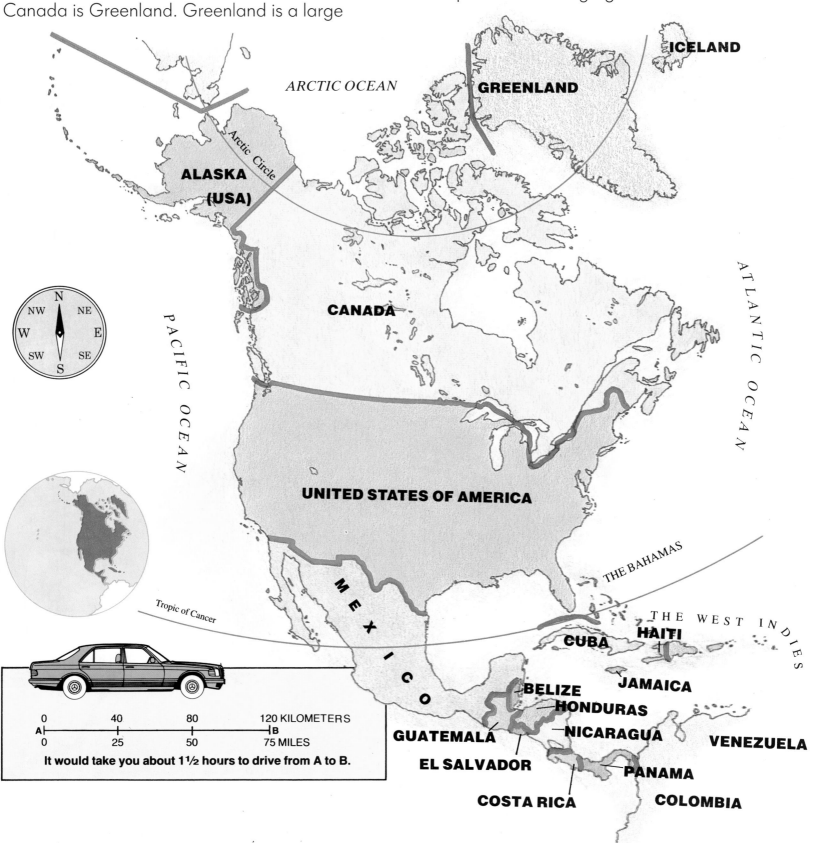

USA
UNITED STATES
OF AMERICA

USA

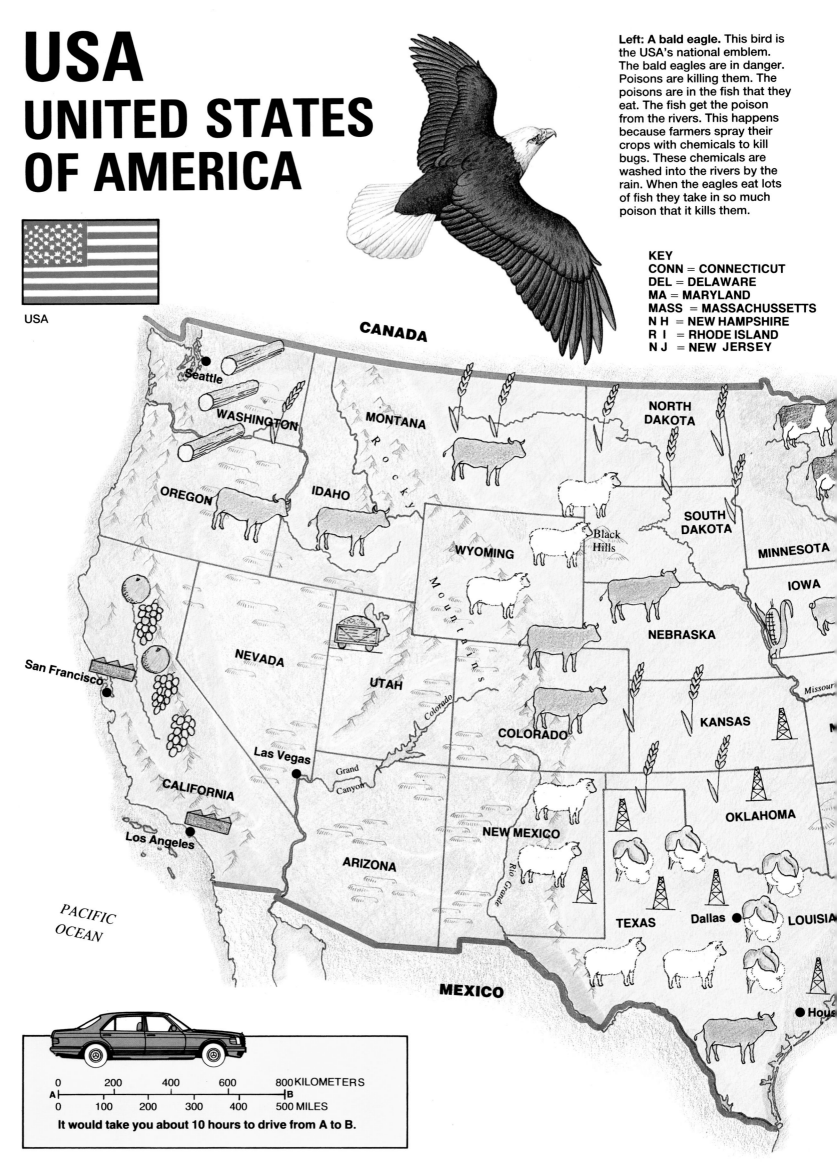

Left: A bald eagle. This bird is the USA's national emblem. The bald eagles are in danger. Poisons are killing them. The poisons are in the fish that they eat. The fish get the poison from the rivers. This happens because farmers spray their crops with chemicals to kill bugs. These chemicals are washed into the rivers by the rain. When the eagles eat lots of fish they take in so much poison that it kills them.

KEY
CONN = CONNECTICUT
DEL = DELAWARE
MA = MARYLAND
MASS = MASSACHUSSETTS
N H = NEW HAMPSHIRE
R I = RHODE ISLAND
N J = NEW JERSEY

CANADA

Seattle

WASHINGTON

MONTANA

NORTH DAKOTA

OREGON

IDAHO

Rocky

SOUTH DAKOTA

MINNESOTA

WYOMING

Black Hills

Mountains

IOWA

San Francisco

NEVADA

UTAH

Colorado

NEBRASKA

Missouri

CALIFORNIA

Las Vegas

Grand Canyon

COLORADO

KANSAS

Los Angeles

ARIZONA

NEW MEXICO

Rio Grande

OKLAHOMA

PACIFIC OCEAN

TEXAS

Dallas

LOUISIA

MEXICO

Hous

0	200	400	600	800 KILOMETERS
A				B
0	100	200	300	400	500 MILES

It would take you about 10 hours to drive from A to B.

The United States of America (USA) is one of the biggest countries in the world. Only three countries are bigger. They are the Soviet Union, Canada and China.

The United States (US) reaches the Pacific Ocean in the west. In the east, it reaches the Atlantic Ocean. New York is on the Atlantic. If you go north from America you will get to Canada. Canada shares the Great Lakes with America. If you go south, you will get to Mexico. Mexico lies on the other side of the Rio Grande. Can you find this river on the map?

Inside America there are many wonderful things to see. There are great mountains, such as the Rocky Mountains in the west. There are highlands, such as the Appalachians in the east. There are wide plains in between.

The Sioux and other Indians used to live here in large tribes. They hunted bison (also called buffalo). Then people came from all over the world to find a new life. Some parts became cowboy country. Corn and cotton were grown in other parts.

There are 48 states together in the main part of America and two other states, Alaska and Hawaii, by themselves. Every state has something special. Texas has lots of oil wells. Many states have mines and factories.

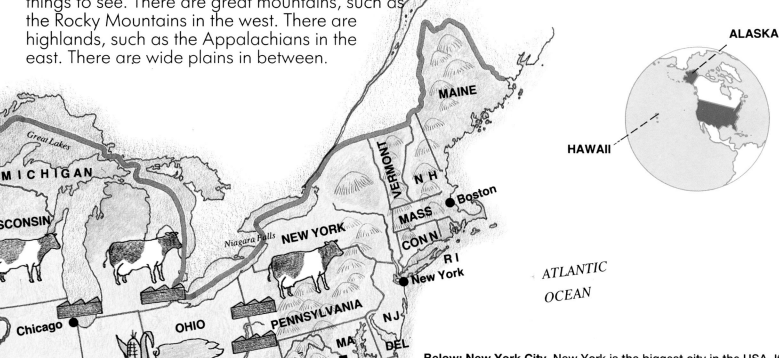

Below: New York City. New York is the biggest city in the USA. It is famous for its tall skyscrapers, like the ones in the picture. Can you find New York City on the map?

CANADA

ARCTIC OCEAN

BAFFIN BAY

QUEEN ELIZABETH ISLANDS

MELVILLE ISLAND

DEVON ISLAND

BANKS ISLAND

BEAUFORT SEA

VICTORIA ISLAND

BAFFIN ISLAND

Arctic Circle

ALASKA (USA)

● Klondike

YUKON TERRITORY

NORTH WEST TERRITORIES

● Yellowknife

PACIFIC OCEAN

BRITISH COLUMBIA

ALBERTA

HUDSON BAY

MANITOBA

SASKATCHEWAN

● Edmonton

● Saskatoon

ONTARIO

VANCOUVER ISLAND

● Vancouver

Prairies

● Winnipeg

USA

● Sud

Great Lakes

0   200   400   600   800 KILOMETERS
A   B
0   100   200   300   400   500 MILES

It would take you about 10 hours to drive from A to B.

20

Canada is a very big country. It is just bigger than America, but not so many people live there. Most people speak English. These families came from England. A lot of families came from France too. They speak French. When the English and French came to Canada, they found many Eskimos and Indians. The Eskimos live in the north. It is very cold there, with much snow and ice.

After the English and French families went to Canada, many Scots, Germans, Poles and others Europeans went there too.

In the cold north, the people dig up rock full of iron, copper and gold. In the rainy west, they catch salmon when the fish swim up the rivers. They also cut down trees to get wood. In the warm, dry south, the people grow wheat and apples, or breed cows for milk. In the stormy east, they catch codfish in the sea.

Canada is now a modern country, with many factories to make things. Canada also has beautiful countryside. Many people go to the Rocky Mountains in the west. Can you find these mountains on the map? There are beautiful lakes here, and great mountains. The mountains have snow and ice on top. There are thick forests all around them.

ATLANTIC OCEAN

NEWFOUNDLAND

NEWFOUNDLAND

St Johns

QUEBEC

Quebec

NEW BRUNSWICK

NOVA SCOTIA

Halifax

Montreal

Ottawa

Toronto

Canada

Left: Maple tree. There are several kinds of maple tree in Canada. One kind of maple tree makes sugar. This is the sugar maple. If you cut its bark, sugar syrup runs out. Canadians, as well as Americans, like to eat pancakes for breakfast, covered with maple syrup. All the maple trees turn to pretty yellows, oranges, reds and purples in the Fall or autumn.

CENTRAL AMERICA AND THE WEST INDIES

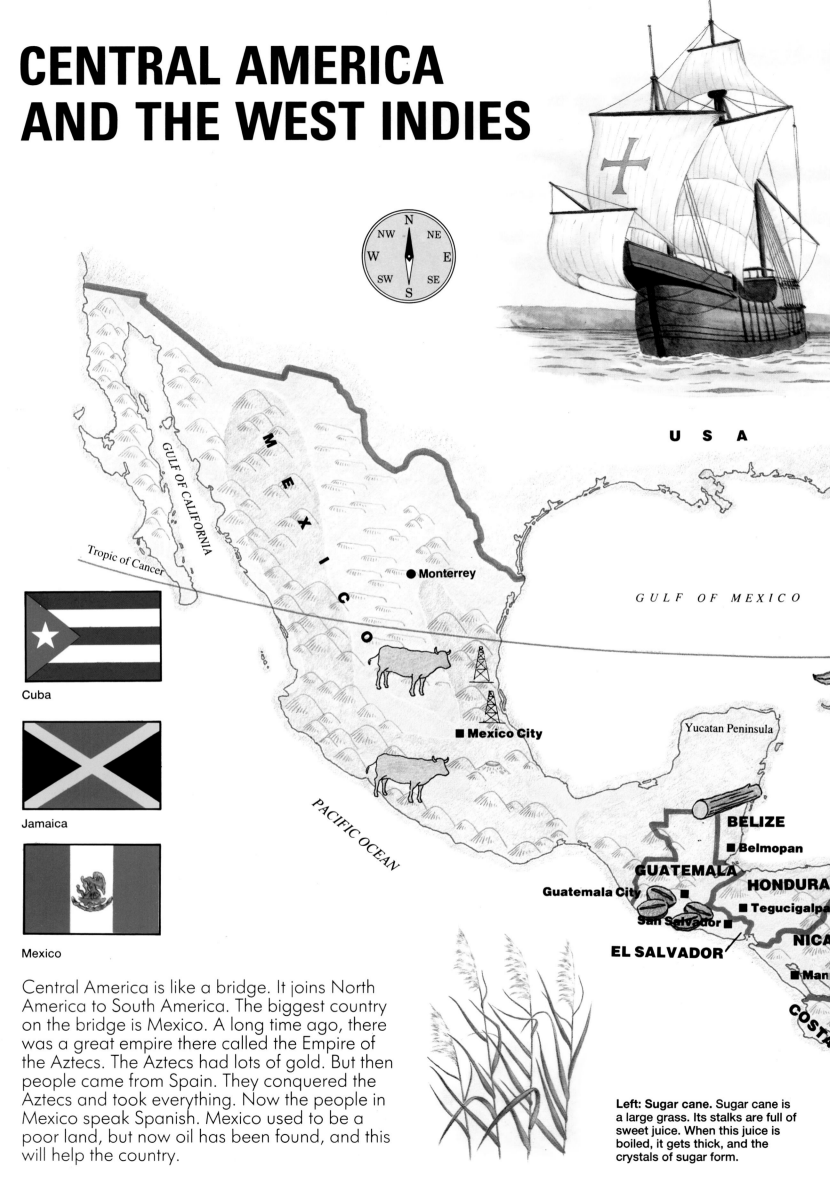

NW N NE
W E
SW S SE

USA

GULF OF CALIFORNIA

M E X I C O

Tropic of Cancer

● Monterrey

GULF OF MEXICO

■ Mexico City

Yucatan Peninsula

PACIFIC OCEAN

BELIZE
■ Belmopan

GUATEMALA
Guatemala City ■

HONDURAS
■ Tegucigalpa

San Salvador ■
EL SALVADOR

NICA
■ Man

COSTA

Cuba

Jamaica

Mexico

Central America is like a bridge. It joins North America to South America. The biggest country on the bridge is Mexico. A long time ago, there was a great empire there called the Empire of the Aztecs. The Aztecs had lots of gold. But then people came from Spain. They conquered the Aztecs and took everything. Now the people in Mexico speak Spanish. Mexico used to be a poor land, but now oil has been found, and this will help the country.

Left: Sugar cane. Sugar cane is a large grass. Its stalks are full of sweet juice. When this juice is boiled, it gets thick, and the crystals of sugar form.

Left: Columbus' ship. Christopher Columbus sailed from Portugal to find America. His brother, Bartholomew, made the maps.

Right: The Panama Canal. The Panama Canal was dug by Spaniards and Italians. They made it so wide and so deep that large ships can go from the Pacific Ocean to the Atlantic Ocean.

ATLANTIC OCEAN

The West Indies is a string of islands. There are big islands such as Cuba, and there are little ones such as Barbados. The natives are called Caribs and Arawaks. They used to own the islands. English, French, Dutch and Spanish people came from Europe a long time ago. They fought each other and then they fought the Caribs and Arawaks. They took the islands, and now the people there speak many languages.

Each island is different. Some are low and made of coral, like the Bahamas. Some are high volcanoes, like Martinique. The islands are very beautiful and it is always warm.

BAHAMAS

■ **Nassau**

Havana
■ **C U B A**

JAMAICA

Port-au-Prince

HAITI **DR**
Santo Domingo

PUERTO RICO
San Juan

ST KITTS
ANTIGUA

KEY
DR = DOMINICAN REPUBLIC
GU = GUADELOUPE
MA = MARTINIQUE

Kingston

GU
DOMINICA
MA

C A R I B B E A N   S E A

ST LUCIA
ST VINCENT
GRENADA

BARBADOS

TRINIDAD AND TOBAGO

UA

COLOMBIA
VENEZUELA

n Jose
Panama Canal

P A N A M A
■ **Panama**

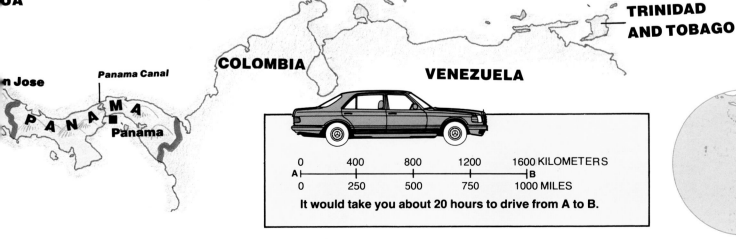

0	400	800	1200	1600 KILOMETERS
A				B
0	250	500	750	1000 MILES

It would take you about 20 hours to drive from A to B.

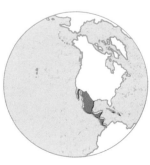

SOUTH AMERICA

South America is a large continent. It lies between the two biggest oceans. To the west is the Pacific Ocean; to the east is the Atlantic Ocean.

All along the Pacific Ocean is a great range of mountains called the Andes. Seven countries share the Andes. Can you see which ones they are?

The first Europeans to come to South America were from Spain and Portugal. Both the Spaniards and the Portuguese took land away from the Indians who lived there. The Portuguese took the land in the east. This is now called Brazil and the people there speak Portuguese. The Spaniards took most of what was left, so most people in South America speak Spanish.

English, French and Dutch people then went to South America. But there was not much land left for them. The English sailed round Cape Horn. Some English and other British sailors got to know the Falkland Islands. They settled there with their families. Their descendants are now mostly shepherds and fishermen.

Brazil is the largest country in South America. It is really a lot of states put together. Brazil has the second longest river in the world: the Amazon. (The longest river in the world is the Nile in Africa.)

Rio de Janeiro is in Brazil. This city is so well known that people often just call it Rio. Rio is famous for its carnival, when everyone sings and dances in the streets.

Many important things come from South America: coffee from Brazil; corned beef from Argentina; oil from Venezuela.

Above: A clearing in the Amazon forest. The Amazon forest is now being cut down to provide timber and grazing land. This is destroying ancient tribes and wildlife and harming the atmosphere. The Amazon basin covers about 2 million square miles. Hundreds of other rivers drain into the Amazon, which is 1,962 miles long.

Left: Ruins of an Inca Palace. The Incas had a great empire in South America some 400 years ago. They built fabulous palaces, temples and forts. Then they were discovered and destroyed by the Spanish Conquistadores.

It would take you about 20 hours to drive from A to B.

CARIBBEAN SEA

TRINIDAD AND TOBAGO

Caracas

VENEZUELA

GUYANA

SURINAM

FRENCH GUIANA

Bogota

COLOMBIA

Equator

Quito

ECUADOR

PERU

Amazon

BRAZIL

Lima

BOLIVIA

Brasilia

PARAGUAY

Rio de Janeiro

Tropic of Capricorn

PACIFIC OCEAN

CHILE

Santiago

Buenos Aires

URUGUAY

ARGENTINA

ATLANTIC OCEAN

N
NW NE
W E
SW SE
S

FALKLAND ISLANDS (UK)

CAPE HORN

Chile

Brazil

Peru

Argentina

25

AUSTRALASIA

Australasia is the name we give to both Australia and New Zealand together. Australia lies between the Indian Ocean in the west and the Pacific Ocean in the east. And it lies between the East Indian Islands in the north and the Antarctic Ocean in the south. The Antarctic Ocean is also called the Southern Ocean.

Australia is made up of seven states: South Australia, Western Australia, Northern Territory, Queensland, New South Wales, Victoria and Tasmania. The first six of these states make a large island. It is the largest island in the world. Tasmania on its own is another island. Australia is as big as the USA and nearly as big as the whole of Europe.

The capital city of Australia is Canberra. (See pages 28-29.) Canberra is not in any state; it has a piece of land all to itself. This is called the Australian Capital Territory.

New Zealand is a pair of islands to the east of Australia: North Island and South Island. (See pages 30-31.)

The capital of New Zealand is Wellington. It is on North Island. Between New Zealand and Australia is the wide Tasman Sea. Tasman and Cook are both names of famous sea captains who discovered these lands.

INDONESIA

TIMOR SEA

INDIAN OCEAN

WESTERN AUSTRALIA

GREAT

Below: An aerial view of Canberra. Canberra is the capital of Australia, though it has fewer people than most American or British cities. The several Australian states couldn't agree about who should have the capital, so Canberra was built.

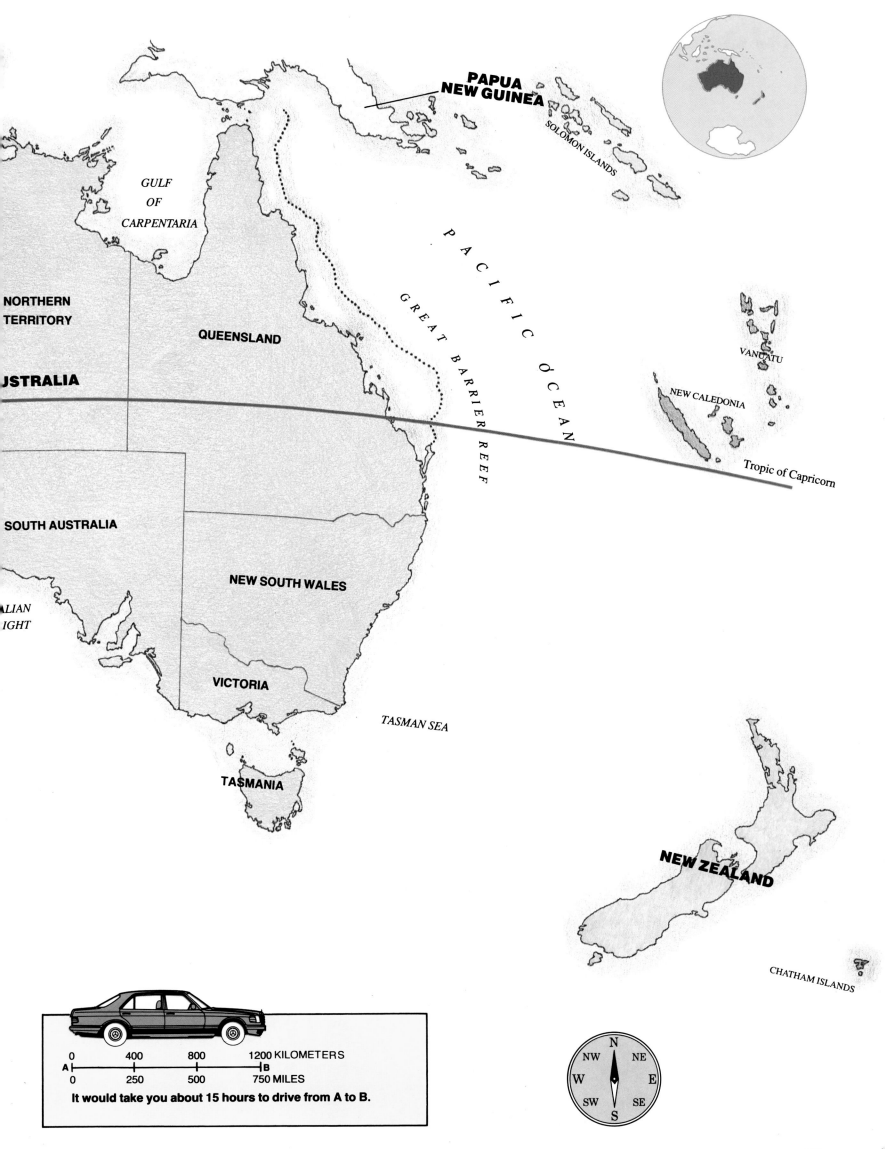

PAPUA
NEW GUINEA

SOLOMON ISLANDS

GULF
OF
CARPENTARIA

P A C I F I C   O C E A N

NORTHERN
TERRITORY

QUEENSLAND

USTRALIA

VANUATU

NEW CALEDONIA

G R E A T   B A R R I E R   R E E F

Tropic of Capricorn

SOUTH AUSTRALIA

NEW SOUTH WALES

LIAN
IGHT

VICTORIA

TASMAN SEA

TASMANIA

NEW ZEALAND

CHATHAM ISLANDS

0	400	800	1200 KILOMETERS
A	250	500	B 750 MILES

It would take you about 15 hours to drive from A to B.

N
NW   NE
W   E
SW   SE
S

AUSTRALIA

Australia is in the southern half of the world. The first people to live here were the Aborigines. Many Europeans have now settled here. The south of the country is towards the South Pole, and is sometimes quite cold. The north of the country is towards the Equator and is sometimes very hot. There are vast deserts here. Can you see them on the map?

Even in the desert it sometimes rains. The rain comes in thunderstorms. All at once, dry valleys become swift rivers. The storm waters pour into Lake Eyre, which grows very big and deep. When the storm is over, all the seeds begin to grow. Within a few days, the desert comes alive with beautiful flowers, and frogs and lizards come out of hiding.

All along the east coast of Australia there is a long line of high mountains. This is called the Great Dividing Range. It catches the rain and so there are forests of tall trees. In many places, the trees have been cut down for timber. This means there is room to grow cane for sugar and to keep cows for milk and beef.

Between the desert and the forests, it is not too dry and not too wet. Grass grows easily here. Wheat is a kind of grass, and so grows well. The farmers also keep lots of sheep for their wool and mutton and lots of cattle for their beef and leather.

Australia is quite a rich country. As well as growing a lot of food, the Australians dig up much iron, gold, copper and coal.

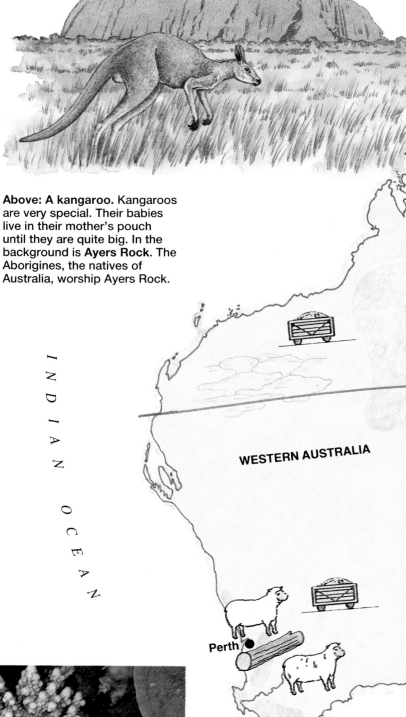

Above: A kangaroo. Kangaroos are very special. Their babies live in their mother's pouch until they are quite big. In the background is **Ayers Rock**. The Aborigines, the natives of Australia, worship Ayers Rock.

INDIAN OCEAN

WESTERN AUSTRALIA

Perth

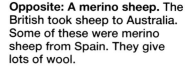

Opposite: A merino sheep. The British took sheep to Australia. Some of these were merino sheep from Spain. They give lots of wool.

Left: Coral and fish of the Great Barrier Reef. The Great Barrier Reef is made of coral reefs. They stick up out of the water and are therefore dangerous to ships. They are made of coral which is hard rock made from the skeletons of sea creatures like sea anemones.

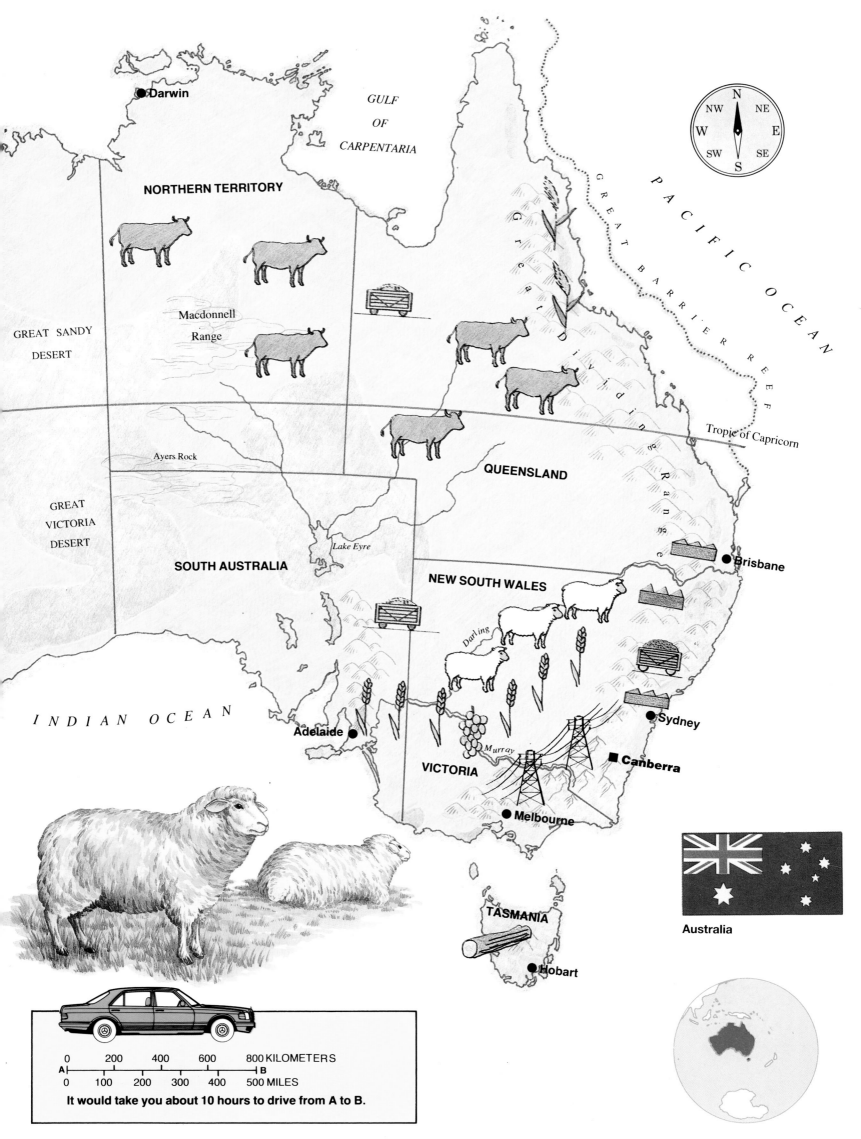

Darwin

GULF
OF
CARPENTARIA

NORTHERN TERRITORY

GREAT SANDY
DESERT

Macdonnell
Range

GREAT
VICTORIA
DESERT

Ayers Rock

Lake Eyre

SOUTH AUSTRALIA

QUEENSLAND

Tropic of Capricorn

GREAT BARRIER REEF

PACIFIC OCEAN

Great Dividing Range

NEW SOUTH WALES

Darling

INDIAN OCEAN

Adelaide

Brisbane

Sydney

Canberra

Murray

VICTORIA

Melbourne

TASMANIA

Hobart

N
NW NE
W E
SW SE
S

Australia

It would take you about 10 hours to drive from A to B.

0   200   400   600   800 KILOMETERS
A|————————————————|B
0   100   200   300   400   500 MILES

NEW ZEALAND

New Zealand

Opposite right: A geyser. Under the ground in Rotorua, in the North Island, the rocks are hot so the water there keeps boiling. Sometimes it spouts high into the air. Then it is called a geyser.

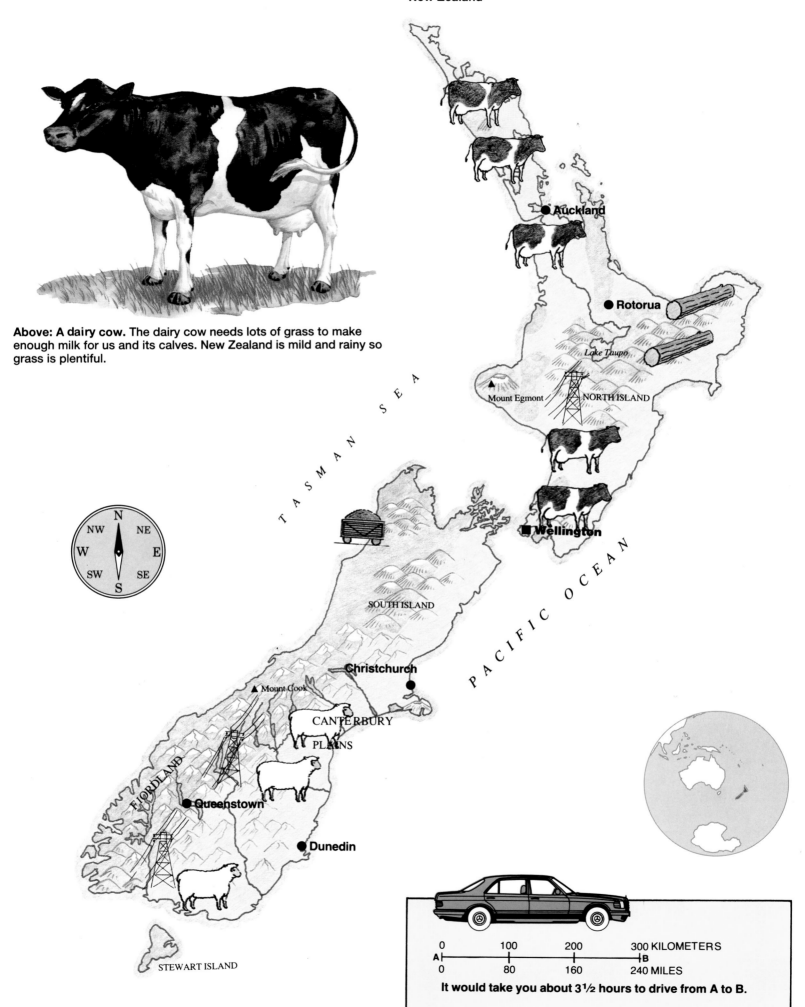

Above: A dairy cow. The dairy cow needs lots of grass to make enough milk for us and its calves. New Zealand is mild and rainy so grass is plentiful.

Auckland

Rotorua

Lake Taupo

Mount Egmont   NORTH ISLAND

TASMAN SEA

Wellington

SOUTH ISLAND

PACIFIC OCEAN

Christchurch

Mount Cook

CANTERBURY PLAINS

FIORDLAND

Queenstown

Dunedin

STEWART ISLAND

0	100	200	300 KILOMETERS
0	80	160	240 MILES

It would take you about 3½ hours to drive from A to B.

The first people to live in New Zealand were the Morioris. They found lots of strange and wonderful things. There were rivers, lakes and fountains of boiling water on North Island. There were lakes, rivers and falls of ice on South Island. And there was a great bird called the moa. It was like a giant ostrich but is extinct now.

About a thousand years ago, more people came to New Zealand. These were the Maoris. They were big and strong, and used to fighting. They soon took the whole of New Zealand for themselves. But a few Morioris survived on the Chatham Islands. Can you find these on the map of Australasia?

Then Captain Cook came to New Zealand. He sailed round the coast about 200 years ago. Can you see any places named after him? Many British families went to New Zealand to become farmers. They fought two great battles against the Maoris. They won both, and so won New Zealand.

The boiling waters round Rotorua attract many visitors. People especially like to see the boiling fountains called geysers.

The ice rivers around Queenstown attract many visitors too. These ice rivers are called glaciers. Some visitors just go sightseeing, but others like to ski.

The North Island has many level plains. Grass grows where the trees were cut down, and the farmers keep dairy cows for butter and cheese. The South Island has a great grassy lowland called the Canterbury Plains. Here, the farmers keep sheep for wool and mutton. These are sold all over the world. New Zealand does not have many factories, so the money it gets for wool and mutton is used to buy things such as cars, clothes and computers.

Below: A kiwi. The kiwi is a very strange bird. It is called a kiwi because it goes 'ki wi, ki wi'. The kiwi came to New Zealand a long time ago. There were no dogs or cats or other animals dangerous to the kiwi in New Zealand then, so over a long time the kiwi began to stop having wings. Now it cannot fly!

THE ANTARCTIC

The Antarctic continent was the last continent to be found and the last to be explored. In a few places, the tops of mountains can be seen. Most of the land is buried under the ice. This is 1 mile thick! Some countries own parts of the Antarctic. These are Britain, Norway, France, Australia and New Zealand. Most of the continent, however, is still not owned by anyone.

The Antarctic Ocean, or Southern Ocean, is all around the continent. Its icy cold waters are full of tiny shrimps called krill, which whales eat. There are not so many whales now, as people have killed most of them.

Above: Captain Scott. Scott reached the South Pole in 1912 but another explorer called Roald Amundsen reached it before him, in December 1911. Most explorers in the Antarctic use sledges pulled by dogs called huskies. A husky's fur is very thick to keep it warm.

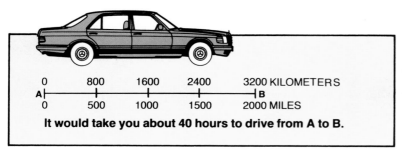

0	800	1600	2400	3200 KILOMETERS
A				B
0	500	1000	1500	2000 MILES

It would take you about 40 hours to drive from A to B.

Below: A penguin. Penguins are birds but they cannot fly. Their wings have turned into flippers. They swim using these flippers when they are catching fish to eat.

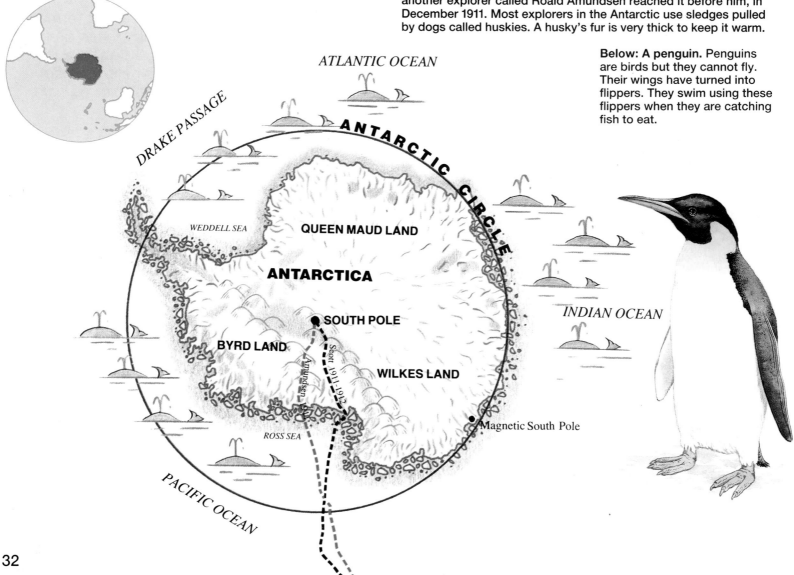

ATLANTIC OCEAN

DRAKE PASSAGE

ANTARCTIC CIRCLE

WEDDELL SEA

QUEEN MAUD LAND

ANTARCTICA

SOUTH POLE

BYRD LAND

Amundsen

Scott 1911 1912

WILKES LAND

INDIAN OCEAN

Magnetic South Pole

ROSS SEA

PACIFIC OCEAN

EUROPE

NW N NE
W E
SW S SE

ARCTIC OCEAN

Arctic Circle

Meridian of Greenwich

SWEDEN

FINLAND

NORWAY

NORTH SEA

REPUBLIC OF IRELAND

UNITED KINGDOM

DENMARK

USSR

NETHERLANDS

BELGIUM

EAST GERMANY

POLAND

ATLANTIC OCEAN

LUXEMBOURG

WEST GERMANY

CZECHOSLOVAKIA

SWITZERLAND

FRANCE

AUSTRIA HUNGARY

ITALY

ROMANIA

PORTUGAL

SPAIN

YUGOSLAVIA

CORSICA

BULGARIA

SARDINIA

ALBANIA

MEDITERRANEAN SEA

GREECE

TURKEY

MOROCCO

ALGERIA

SICILY

CRETE

0   400   800   1200   1600 KILOMETERS
A |----|----|----|----| B
0   250   500   750   1000 MILES

It would take you about 20 hours to drive from A to B.

We call Europe a continent because it is very important. But Europe is joined on to Asia. It isn't really a continent on its own. Europe goes as far north as the Arctic Ocean, as far west as the Atlantic Ocean and as far east as the Ural Mountains.

Many countries in Europe used to have great empires. They kept fighting each other and everyone else. Even Denmark had an empire and still owns Greenland. Russia has got the whole of the north of Asia.

The British Empire was the biggest. British sailors, soldiers, traders and rulers went all over the world. The British Empire is now broken up into separate countries, but some of them are part of the British Commonwealth.

There have been two world wars that started in Europe. The Europeans are trying to stop arguing with one another. They want to help each other instead. Some countries have joined together to form the European Economic Community (E.E.C.).

THE BRITISH ISLES

Long ago, during the Ice Age, the British Isles were covered by ice. When the ice melted, trees began to grow, and deer ran in the forests. Then the Britons went across the English Channel to settle there. Their descendants are called the Irish, Scots and Welsh, and they have their own countries. The English arrived later, and their country is England.

Ireland has lots of marshes and bogs. It is famous for its dairy cows, but there is enough good ground to grow potatoes and barley. Northern Ireland is also known for making ships and linen.

Scotland has many mountains which attract tourists. Scotland is also famous for oil and whisky. Wales is also mountainous but is better known for its deep valleys. These valleys cut down into thick seams of coal. Many Welshmen are miners. The coal is used to make iron and steel.

England is mostly hills and valleys; there are few mountains so farming is very easy. The English found lots of coal and ironstone. They invented ways to make iron and steel very quickly and cheaply. Then they invented machines to spin and weave cloth. This introduction of machines to do work was called the Industrial Revolution.

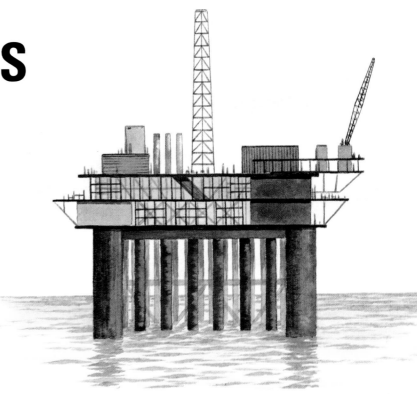

Above: An oil platform. From here drills are sent down into the ground to get oil. There is a great deal of oil under the North Sea.

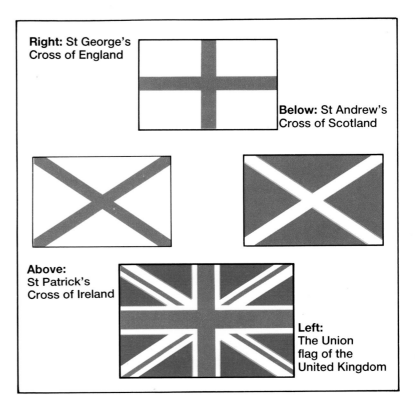

Right: St George's Cross of England

Below: St Andrew's Cross of Scotland

Above: St Patrick's Cross of Ireland

Left: The Union flag of the United Kingdom

Right: The flags of the United Kingdom. The Union Flag is made up of three flags on top of one another, starting with the flag of St George, the patron saint of England. The word Union means the union or joining of England, Wales, Scotland and Northern Ireland to become the United Kingdom. The Union Flag is usually called the Union Jack. Jack means jacket or coat, and the old crusaders used to wear the flag on their coats.

Below: Breakdown of the British Isles: The British Isles is made up of England, Scotland, Wales, Northern Ireland, the Republic of Ireland and all the little islands. The United Kingdom is England, Scotland, Wales and Northern Ireland. Great Britain is England, Wales and Scotland. The Republic of Ireland is a separate country and has its own flag.

The British Isles

The United Kingdom

Great Britain

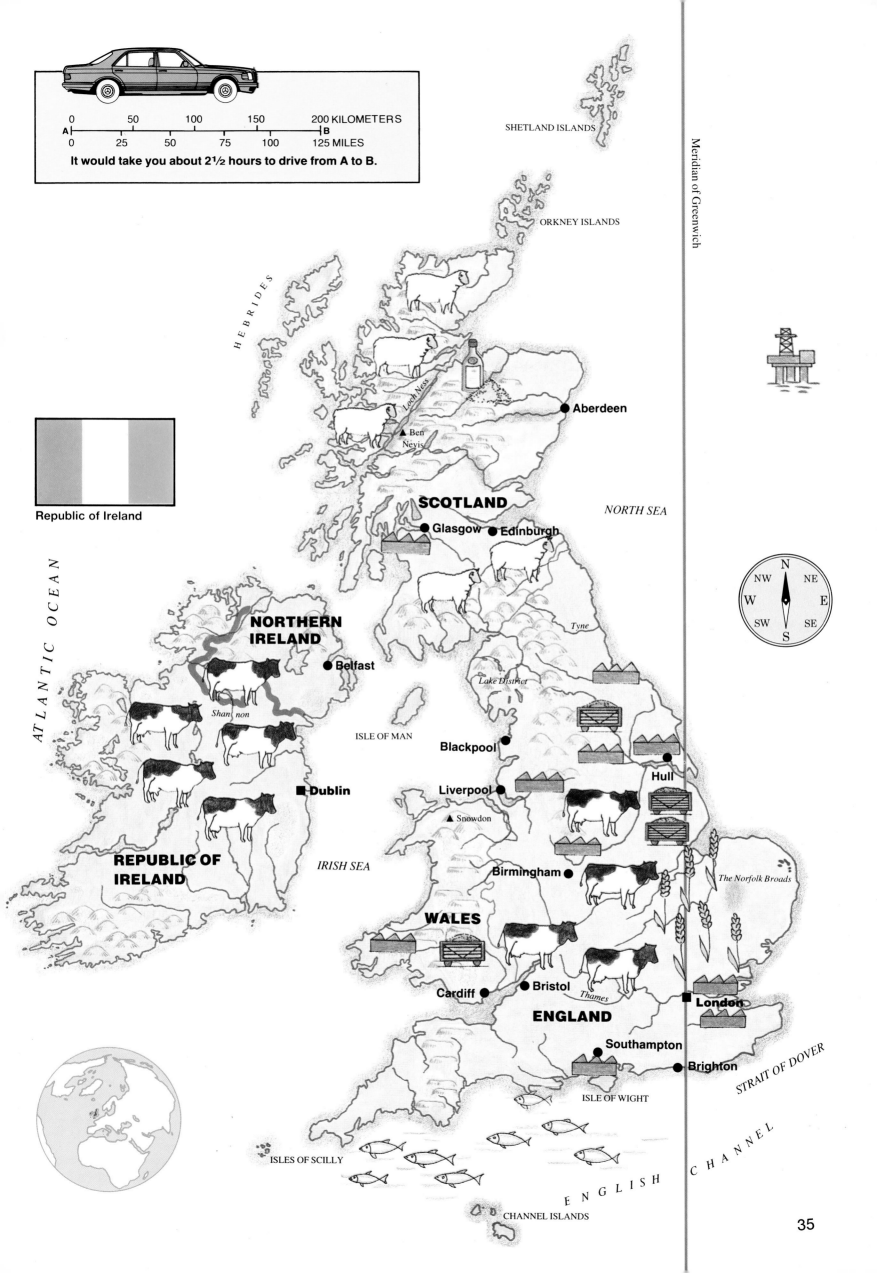

0   50   100   150   200 KILOMETERS

A |————————————————| B

0   25   50   75   100   125 MILES

It would take you about 2½ hours to drive from A to B.

SHETLAND ISLANDS

Meridian of Greenwich

ORKNEY ISLANDS

HEBRIDES

Loch Ness

● Aberdeen

▲ Ben Nevis

SCOTLAND

NORTH SEA

● Glasgow   ● Edinburgh

Republic of Ireland

ATLANTIC OCEAN

Tyne

NORTHERN IRELAND

● Belfast

Shannon

Lake District

ISLE OF MAN

● Blackpool

Hull

■ Dublin

● Liverpool

▲ Snowdon

REPUBLIC OF IRELAND

IRISH SEA

Birmingham ●

The Norfolk Broads

WALES

Thames

Cardiff ●   ● Bristol

■ London

ENGLAND

Southampton ●

Brighton ●

STRAIT OF DOVER

ISLE OF WIGHT

ISLES OF SCILLY

E N G L I S H   C H A N N E L

CHANNEL ISLANDS

N
NW   NE
W   E
SW   SE
S

35

THE ENGLISH CHANNEL AND ITS NEIGHBORS

The English Channel is one of the most important seaways in the world. It is so well known that we often just call it the Channel. The Channel joins the Atlantic Ocean to the North Sea. Can you find the Strait of Dover? It is very narrow there and ships have to be careful not to hit one another.

A long time ago, boatloads of men and their families sailed across the Channel and the North Sea to Britain. These invaders were from tribes of farmers who wanted more land. Some of them were Norsemen. The Norsemen also went to France and called it Normandy. William was their king. He took his army across the Channel and conquered all England. This was the Norman Conquest, and after that, William was called William the Conqueror.

There are many ferry boats going across the Channel. Tourists from France like to go to London to see Buckingham Palace and St Paul's Cathedral. British tourists like to go across to Paris to see the Eiffel Tower and the Pompidou Center. When British people go to France, they often say that they are going to the Continent. They forget that the whole of the British Isles is really part of the continent.

The British and the French have got together to build a great tunnel under the Channel. We often call this Channel Tunnel "the Chunnel"! There will actually be two tunnels, side by side. Both will have trains running through them. It will be one of the greatest ever building feats.

ATLANTIC OCEAN

WALES

● Bristol

● Plymouth

E N G L I S H

CHANNEL ISLANDS

Left: The Concorde. The Concorde is the world's first supersonic passenger-carrying aircraft. It was designed and built by the British and the French and travels faster than the speed of sound. It gains its name from the English and French word, concord(e), which means helping and agreeing with one another.

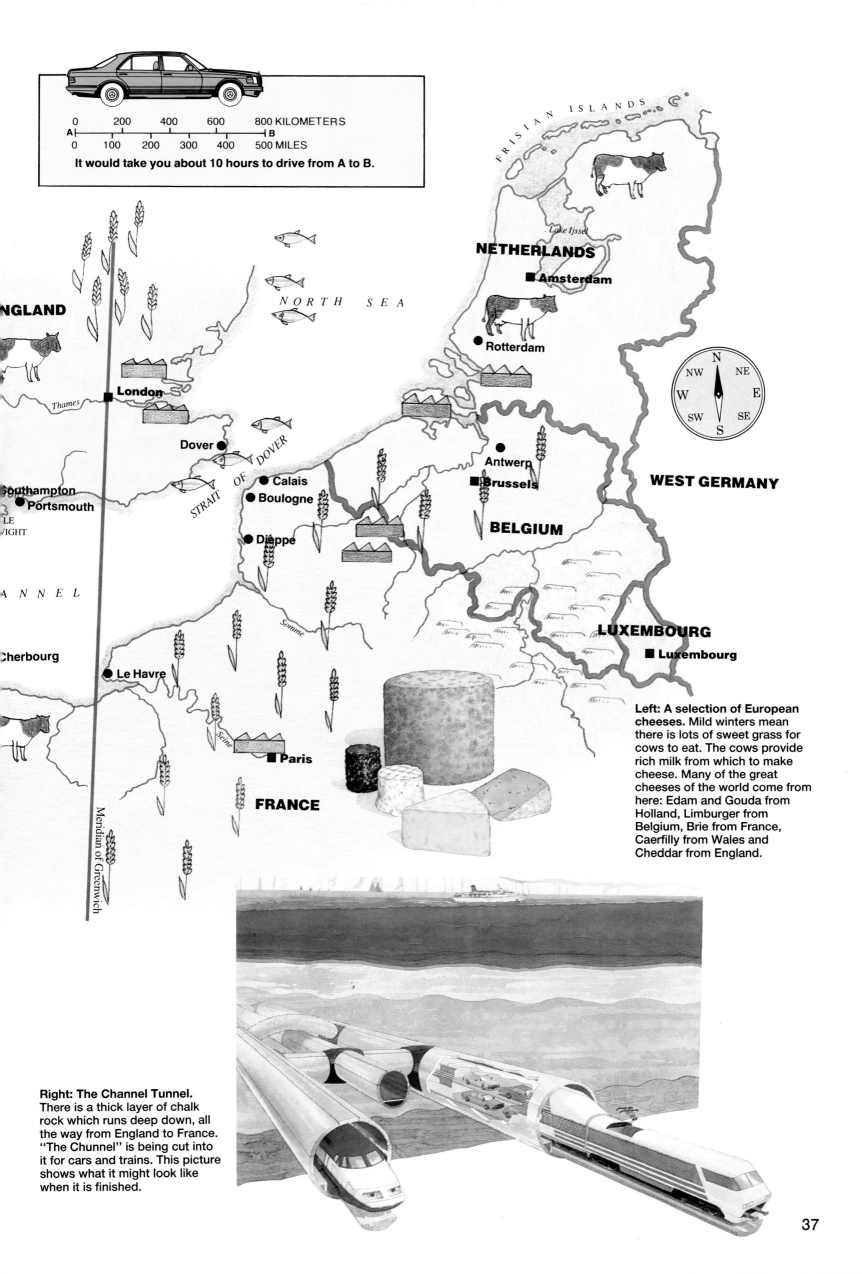

It would take you about 10 hours to drive from A to B.

FRISIAN ISLANDS

NORTH SEA

NETHERLANDS
■ Amsterdam

Lake Ijssel

● Rotterdam

NW N NE
W E
SW S SE

WEST GERMANY

ENGLAND

Thames

■ London

Dover ●

Southampton
● Portsmouth
LE
IGHT

STRAIT OF DOVER

● Calais
● Boulogne

● Dieppe

● Antwerp
■ Brussels

BELGIUM

LUXEMBOURG
■ Luxembourg

HANNEL

Cherbourg

● Le Havre

Somme

Seine

■ Paris

FRANCE

Meridian of Greenwich

Left: A selection of European cheeses. Mild winters mean there is lots of sweet grass for cows to eat. The cows provide rich milk from which to make cheese. Many of the great cheeses of the world come from here: Edam and Gouda from Holland, Limburger from Belgium, Brie from France, Caerfilly from Wales and Cheddar from England.

Right: The Channel Tunnel. There is a thick layer of chalk rock which runs deep down, all the way from England to France. "The Chunnel" is being cut into it for cars and trains. This picture shows what it might look like when it is finished.

FRANCE, SPAIN AND PORTUGAL

There has been a country called France for a long time. The French used to have a large empire. Now they have only Corsica, French Guiana and a few tiny islands far away.

In the old days, France and other European countries were always fighting. The French were protected from the Spaniards because they were separated by great mountains called the Pyrenees. Some more mountains, the Alps, protected the French from the Italians. But in the northeast the land is low. Sometimes foreign armies came in here to attack the French; sometimes the French armies left France from here.

Farming is very important in France. The people in France make good wine and cheese and grow most of their own food. There are also many mines and factories. People from other countries often go to France for holidays.

France

Spain

Portugal

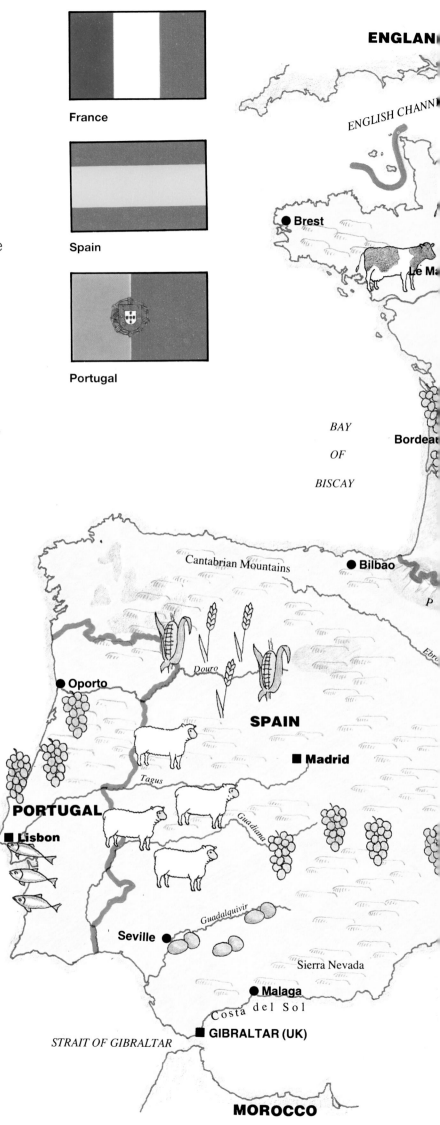

ENGLAN

ENGLISH CHANN

● Brest

Le Ma

BAY

OF

BISCAY

Bordea

Cantabrian Mountains

● Bilbao

P

Ebro

Douro

Oporto

SPAIN

■ Madrid

Tagus

PORTUGAL

Guadiana

■ Lisbon

Guadalquivir

Seville ●

Sierra Nevada

● Malaga

Costa del Sol

STRAIT OF GIBRALTAR

■ GIBRALTAR (UK)

MOROCCO

Above: A grape vine. Grapes grow in bunches on plants called vines. Grapes are good to eat and wine is made out of them. Other kinds of vines give us currants, and brown and golden raisins.

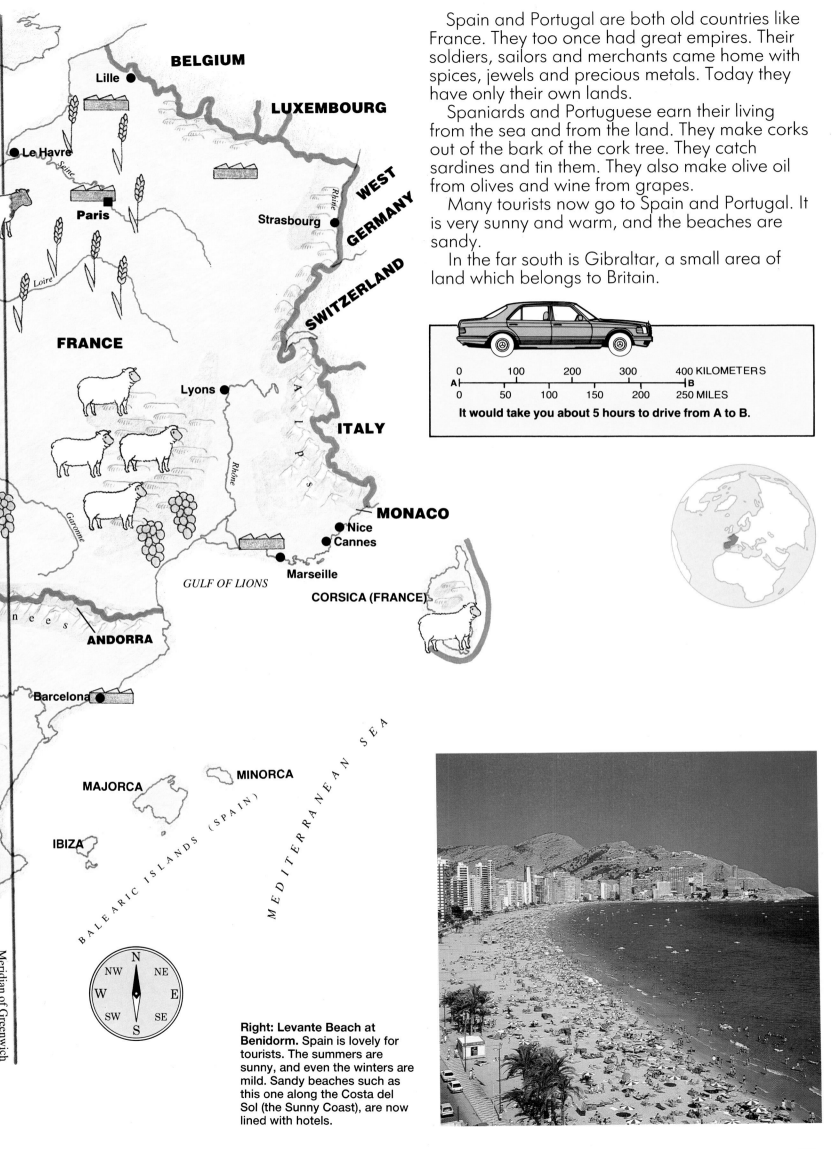

Spain and Portugal are both old countries like France. They too once had great empires. Their soldiers, sailors and merchants came home with spices, jewels and precious metals. Today they have only their own lands.

Spaniards and Portuguese earn their living from the sea and from the land. They make corks out of the bark of the cork tree. They catch sardines and tin them. They also make olive oil from olives and wine from grapes.

Many tourists now go to Spain and Portugal. It is very sunny and warm, and the beaches are sandy.

In the far south is Gibraltar, a small area of land which belongs to Britain.

| 0 | 100 | 200 | 300 | 400 KILOMETERS |
| 0 | 50 | 100 | 150 | 200 | 250 MILES |

It would take you about 5 hours to drive from A to B.

BELGIUM

Lille

LUXEMBOURG

Le Havre

WEST GERMANY

Paris

Strasbourg

SWITZERLAND

FRANCE

Lyons

ITALY

MONACO

Nice
Cannes

Marseille

GULF OF LIONS

CORSICA (FRANCE)

ANDORRA

Barcelona

MAJORCA

MINORCA

IBIZA

BALEARIC ISLANDS (SPAIN)

MEDITERRANEAN SEA

Rhine

Seine

Loire

Garonne

Rhône

P y r e n e e s

A l p s

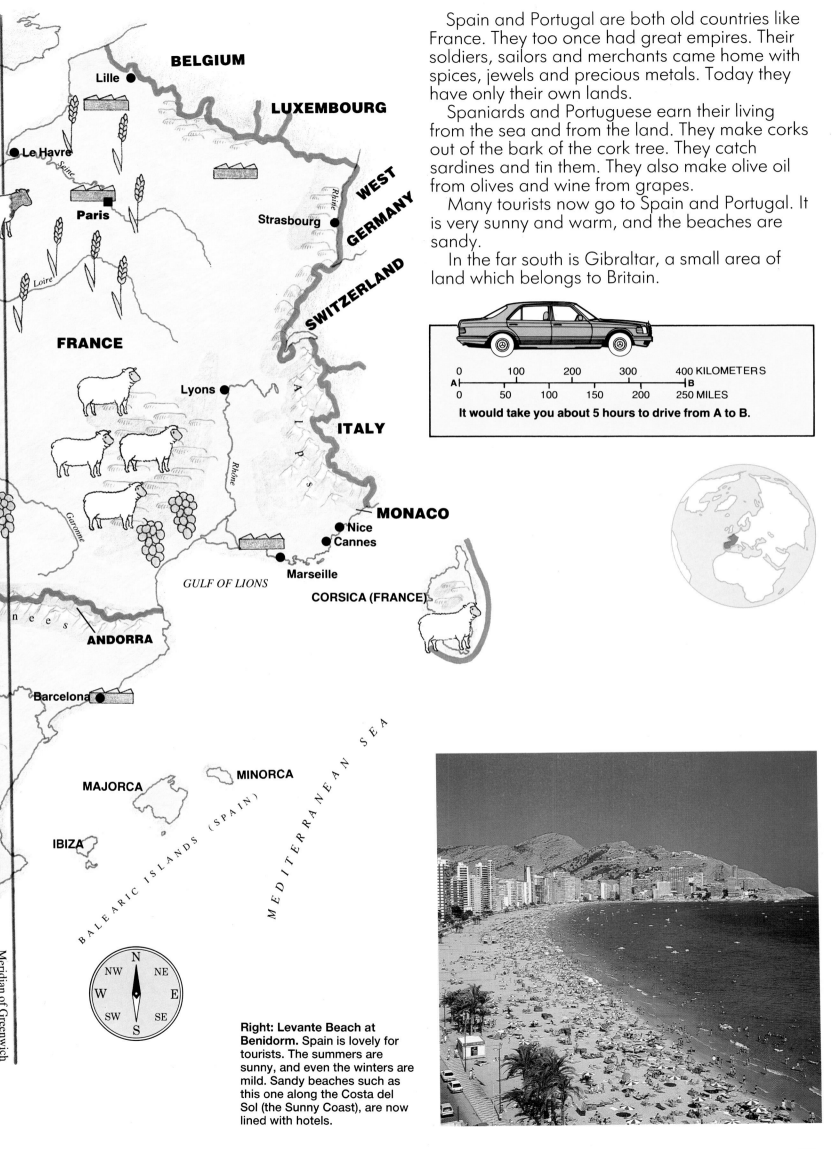

N
NW NE
W E
SW SE
S

Right: Levante Beach at Benidorm. Spain is lovely for tourists. The summers are sunny, and even the winters are mild. Sandy beaches such as this one along the Costa del Sol (the Sunny Coast), are now lined with hotels.

Meridian of Greenwich

39

ITALY, GREECE AND THEIR NEIGHBORS

CZECHOSLOVAKIA

WEST GERMANY

AUSTRIA

Vienna ■

■ Budapest

HUNGARY

Lake Constance

Rhine

■ Berne

SWITZERLAND

Lake Geneva

● Geneva

▲ Matterhorn

FRANCE

Milan ●

● Venice

Genoa ●

● Belgrade

ADRIATIC SEA

● Florence

YUGOSLAVIA

CORSICA
(FRANCE)

Appenine

TYRRHENIAN SEA

Rome ■

Mountains

● Naples

ITALY

■ Tirana

ALBANIA

SARDINIA
(ITALY)

IONIAN SEA

GREECE

SICILY
(ITALY)

MEDITERRANEAN

MALTA

Italy

Greece

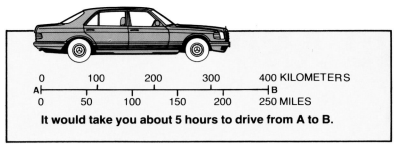

0 100 200 300 400 KILOMETERS
A ├─────────────────────────────────┤ B
0 50 100 150 200 250 MILES

It would take you about 5 hours to drive from A to B.

Right: The Parthenon. There are many ruins like this one in Greece. The Parthenon was built as a temple to pray to the goddess, Athena. It did not fall down into ruins just because it was old. Like most ruins, people stole pieces of it to build something else.

Carpathian Mountains

ROMANIA

USSR

Transylvanian Alps

Danube

■ Bucharest

BULGARIA

BLACK SEA

■ Sofia

TURKEY

TURKEY

AEGEAN SEA

■ Athens

CYPRUS

A

CRETE (GREECE)

Italy and Greece jut out into the Mediterranean Sea. They are called peninsulas. Italy is long and narrow and Greece is short and fat.

Greece is very mountainous but has many small, low, level plains between the mountains. The plain around Athens is the most famous. The soil is fertile, the winters are mild and the summers are hot and sunny. All this is good for growing grapes for wine, olives for olive oil and wheat for bread.

People have lived in Greece for a very long time. Hundreds of years ago Greek sailors and soldiers went out to take more land, and to make a great empire. Greek merchants went out to build city-ports all round the Mediterranean Sea. Here they bought food and sold Greek crockery, tableware, lamps and lots of other things.

The Greek Empire broke up. It was taken over by the Roman Empire. The capital city of Italy is still called Rome.

The Roman Empire became too large to look after and Rome (Italy) broke up into lots of tiny countries. Each had one big, famous city, like Venice or Genoa or Florence. Although small, these were rich and full of great churches and famous artists. Now Italy is one country again.

Today, millions of tourists go to Italy and Greece. Yugoslavia, Hungary and Romania now get a lot of tourists too, but Albania is a very private country and it is difficult to go there.

Switzerland has many very high mountains. These are called the Alps. They are the highest mountains in Europe and many people go there to ski on the snowy slopes. Austria also has a share of the Alps.

41

GERMANY, POLAND AND CZECHOSLOVAKIA

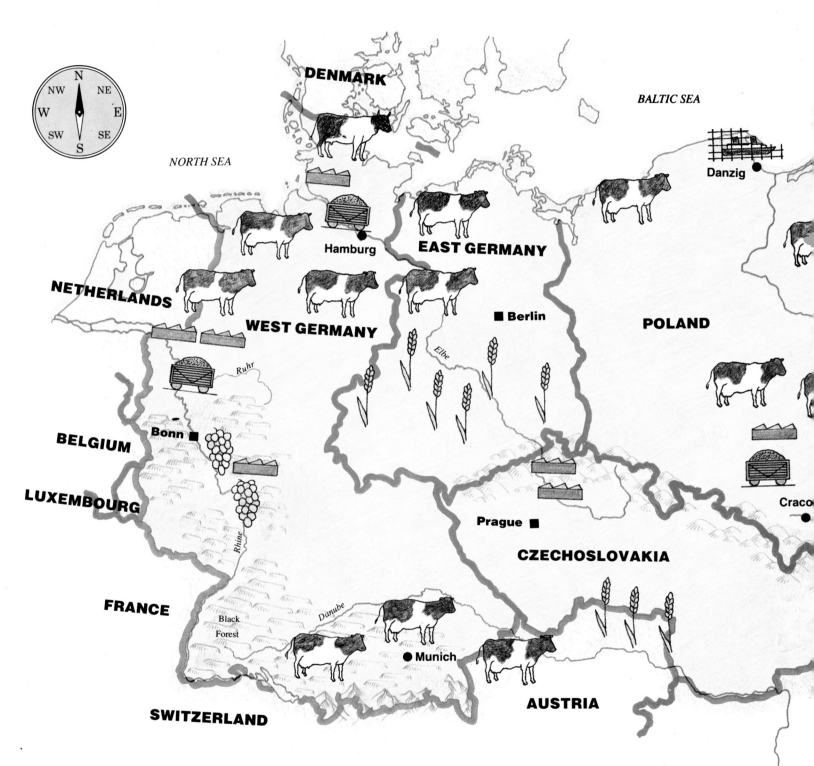

Long ago in this part of Europe, there were no separate countries and no cities. There were just some tribes of farmers who often fought each other. They wanted more and more land for their large families. So some went to England and are now English. But most of them went eastwards, across what is now called Poland, and into what is now called the USSR.

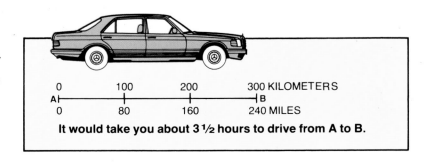

It would take you about 3 ½ hours to drive from A to B.

Left: Shipbuilding. Germany and Poland build many ships near Hamburg and Danzig. They build liners for tourists, tankers for oil, freighters for cargo and trawlers for fishermen.

Warsaw

Vistula

USSR

rpathian Mountains

HUNGARY

West Germany

Poland

Czechoslovakia

Later on, frontiers were made between the tribes, and that is how countries began. Where most people spoke German, it became Germany. Poland was where most people spoke Polish. Russia (now called the USSR) was where most people spoke Russian. Czechoslovakia is quite a new country. There are two different groups of people – the Czechs and the Slovaks and they each speak a different language.

The Germans had no empire but the people were full of ideas and energy. They invented many things and built enormous factories to make all kinds of things out of metals and chemicals. The biggest area of factories is the Ruhr. In the Ruhr area they make many things including cloth, engines and fertilizers.

Poland used to have a big empire, but much of the land it had has been taken by other countries. There is coal and copper in Poland and many ships are made there.

Right: Checkpoint Charlie on the Berlin Wall. The Berlin Wall goes across the city of Berlin. It separates East Berlin from West Berlin. East Berlin is the capital of East Germany but West Berlin belongs to West Germany. People can cross the wall at gates such as Checkpoint Charlie.

SCANDINAVIA

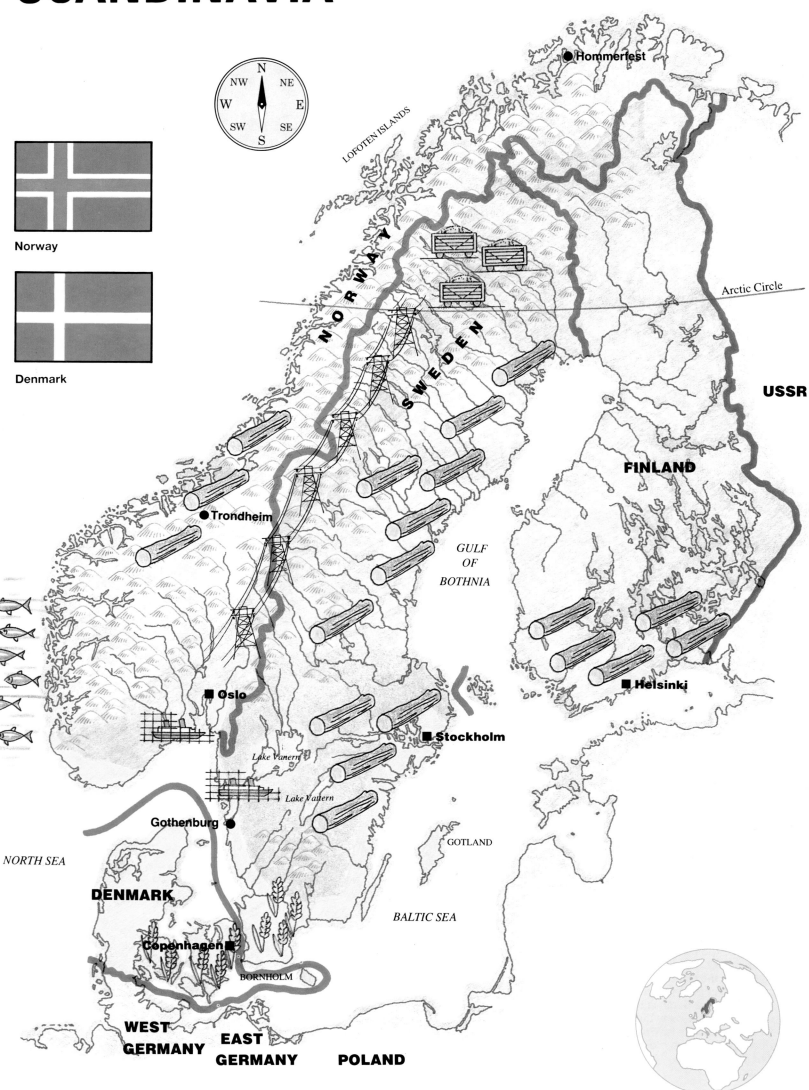

ARCTIC OCEAN

● **Hommerfest**

LOFOTEN ISLANDS

Norway

Denmark

Arctic Circle

USSR

N
O
R
W
A
Y

S
W
E
D
E
N

● **Trondheim**

FINLAND

*GULF
OF
BOTHNIA*

■ **Oslo**

■ **Helsinki**

Lake Vanern

■ **Stockholm**

Lake Vattern

Gothenburg ●

GOTLAND

NORTH SEA

DENMARK

BALTIC SEA

Copenhagen ■

BORNHOLM

**WEST
GERMANY**

**EAST
GERMANY**

POLAND

Above: Fishing off Norway. Norway's cool water is full of fish. Cod swim in the depths and herrings near the surface. Norway is well-known for its fishing industry.

When people talk about Scandinavia, they sometimes mean just Norway and Sweden, and sometimes they mean Finland and Denmark as well. Norway and Sweden are very mountainous. In some parts the mountains are very high and have snow and ice all year. In other parts the land is still high but flat on top. Heather, moss and lichen can grow when the snow melts, and so there is food for reindeer.

Lower down the mountains, there are forests of tall trees. Their wood is good for making into floors, boxes, doors and even paper.

When the snow and ice melts, it rushes down the rivers. The fast water turns giant propellers called turbines to make electricity.

Finland is forested, just like Norway and Sweden, but it is much lower and flatter. Therefore there are thousands of large and small lakes. Nearly half of Finland is covered by water! People can skate on the lakes in winter and fish in them in summer.

Norway, Sweden and Finland were all covered by a great sheet of ice during the Ice Age. The ice scraped away most of the soil, and so it is hard to grow food in these countries. The ice slowly moved to Denmark, where it melted. It dropped all the soil onto Denmark so the Danes can grow lush, sweet grass for cows. These are dairy cows; their milk is made into butter, cream and cheese. Some of the grass is given to pigs, and Denmark is famous for ham and bacon.

Below: A reindeer. The Lapps, who live in the northern forests of Scandinavia, follow the reindeer to get their meat, milk, leather and fur. So the reindeer give food, drink and clothes.

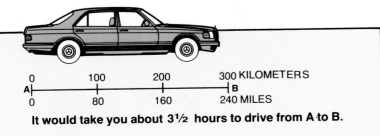

0   100   200   300 KILOMETERS
A|————|————|————|B
0   80   160   240 MILES

It would take you about 3½ hours to drive from A to B.

USSR

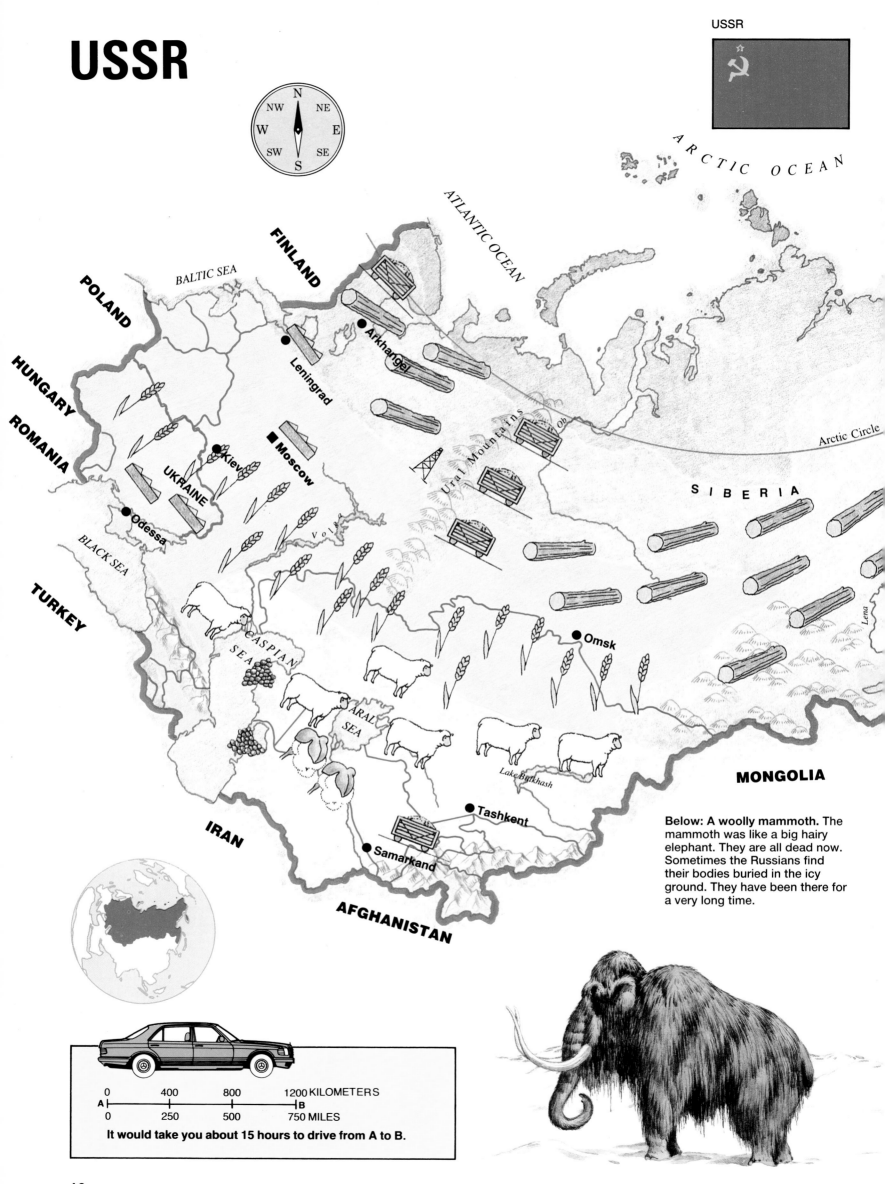

USSR

ARCTIC OCEAN

ATLANTIC OCEAN

FINLAND

BALTIC SEA

POLAND

HUNGARY

ROMANIA

● Arkhangel

● Leningrad

■ Moscow

● Kiev

UKRAINE

● Odessa

BLACK SEA

TURKEY

Volga

CASPIAN SEA

ARAL SEA

Ural Mountains

Ob

Arctic Circle

SIBERIA

Lena

● Omsk

Lake Balkhash

MONGOLIA

IRAN

● Tashkent

● Samarkand

AFGHANISTAN

Below: A woolly mammoth. The mammoth was like a big hairy elephant. They are all dead now. Sometimes the Russians find their bodies buried in the icy ground. They have been there for a very long time.

0	400	800	1200 KILOMETERS
0	250	500	750 MILES

A ⊢ ⊣ B

It would take you about 15 hours to drive from A to B.

The full name of the USSR is the Union of Soviet Socialist Republics. It is often just called Russia. It is really a kind of united states like the United States of America, but it is called a union instead of united and its states are called republics.

Part of the USSR is in Europe and part is in Asia. Europe and Asia are separated by the Ural Mountains. Can you see these mountains on the map?

All kinds of people live in the USSR and they have strange names such as Ostyaks, Samoyeds and Uzbeks. There are also many Jews and the great, great grandchildren of Germans who went there long, long ago. At that time, there weren't any real countries; there were just a lot of tribes of people trying to stay alive.

Then the true Russians around Moscow made themselves into a country. They wanted to make a great empire and get rich. The Russians couldn't go north because of the Arctic Ocean, but they could go east. Thousands of Russian families left the Moscow area. They crossed over the Ural Mountains and went right across Siberia to the Pacific Ocean. Just as the pioneers in America went west into Indian country, so the pioneers in Russia went east into lands where Mongols, Yukaghirs and other tribes lived. All along the route, the Russians started farms to grow wheat and cabbages. They felled trees to build houses and to make paper.

The old rulers of Russia were called czars and czarinas. They wanted Russia to be a modern country with mines, railways and factories. British people were already making these so the czars paid the British to show them what to do.

Below: These two photographs show two kinds of Russian people. They look very different.
Left: A market in Samarkand. In this part of Russia it can get very hot. And it can get very cold in winter.
Right: May Day in Leningrad. People all over the world celebrate 1 May. The Russians celebrate communism. In other countries people celebrate spring.

THE ARCTIC

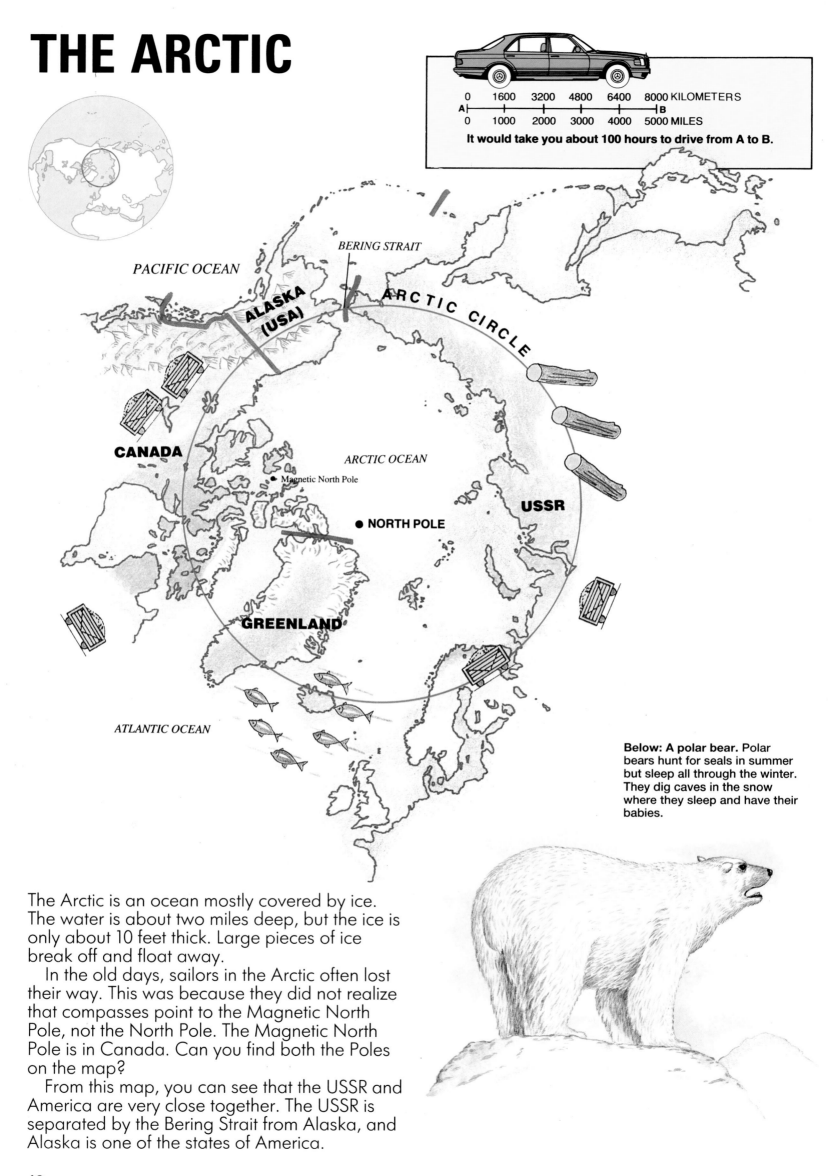

0   1600   3200   4800   6400   8000 KILOMETERS
A├──────┼──────┼──────┼──────┼──────┤B
0   1000   2000   3000   4000   5000 MILES

It would take you about 100 hours to drive from A to B.

PACIFIC OCEAN

BERING STRAIT

ALASKA (USA)

ARCTIC CIRCLE

CANADA

ARCTIC OCEAN

Magnetic North Pole

● NORTH POLE

USSR

GREENLAND

ATLANTIC OCEAN

Below: A polar bear. Polar bears hunt for seals in summer but sleep all through the winter. They dig caves in the snow where they sleep and have their babies.

The Arctic is an ocean mostly covered by ice. The water is about two miles deep, but the ice is only about 10 feet thick. Large pieces of ice break off and float away.

In the old days, sailors in the Arctic often lost their way. This was because they did not realize that compasses point to the Magnetic North Pole, not the North Pole. The Magnetic North Pole is in Canada. Can you find both the Poles on the map?

From this map, you can see that the USSR and America are very close together. The USSR is separated by the Bering Strait from Alaska, and Alaska is one of the states of America.

THE GULF

A gulf is part of the sea which goes deep into the land. This gulf is so well known that we often call it, simply, the Gulf. It lies between Saudi Arabia to the southwest and Iran to the northeast. Iran used to be called Persia and there was once a great Persian empire. Persian ships sailed all over the Gulf, so it was called the Persian Gulf. The empire broke up and new rulers called shahs came.

People found oil and gas in all the countries round the Gulf. They put oil wells on the land and in the water. Soon this became the most important part of the world for oil. Kuwait has enough oil underground to last for 200 years. Bahrain is just a little island, but with oil under water. Can you find Bahrain on the map?

Below: Oil production in the Gulf. The oil that comes out of the ground is a mixture of many different kinds. These have to be separated in a refinery. That is how we get diesel oil for trucks, petrol for cars and paraffin for tractors, and camping gas. (Petrol is also called gasolene; paraffin is also called kerosene.) Sometimes there is so much gas at the refinery that it is just burnt off!

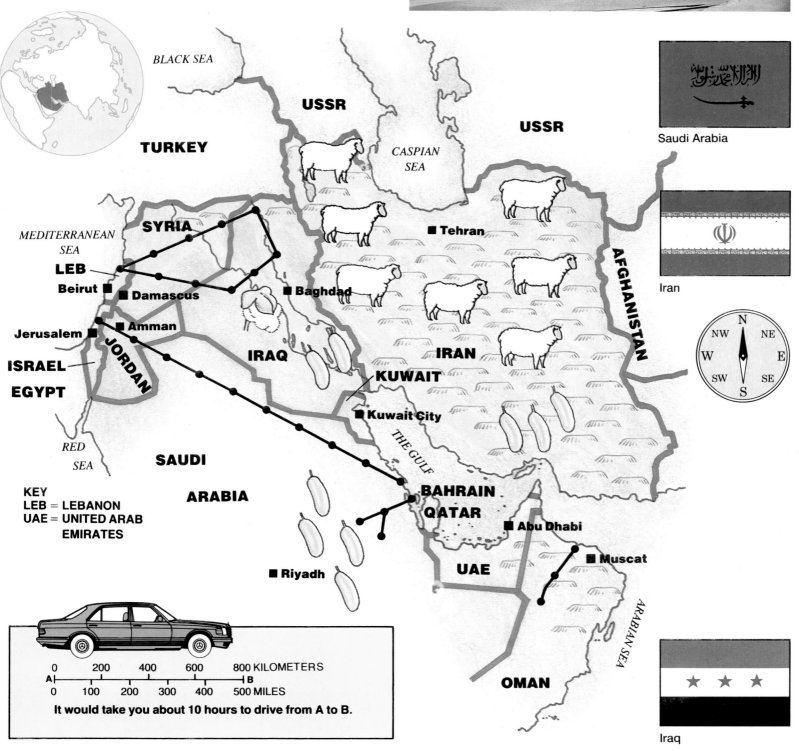

KEY
LEB = LEBANON
UAE = UNITED ARAB
EMIRATES

0   200   400   600   800 KILOMETERS
A├───┼───┼───┼───┤B
0   100   200   300   400   500 MILES
It would take you about 10 hours to drive from A to B.

Saudi Arabia

Iran

Iraq

THE MIDDLE EAST AND INDIA

The Middle East is often in the news. Iran, Iraq, Israel and the Lebanon are all in the Middle East. Jesus was born in Bethlehem, near Jerusalem; Mohammed was born in Mecca. Millions of pilgrims go to Jerusalem and to Mecca every year. Can you find these two cities on the map?

India is a large country between the Arabian Sea and the Bay of Bengal. It used to be part of the British Empire. It was even larger then. The people living in the northwest wanted their own country so the country called Pakistan was formed there. The people in the northeast also wanted their own country so Bangladesh was formed. South of India there is an island which is also now an independent country. It is called Sri Lanka.

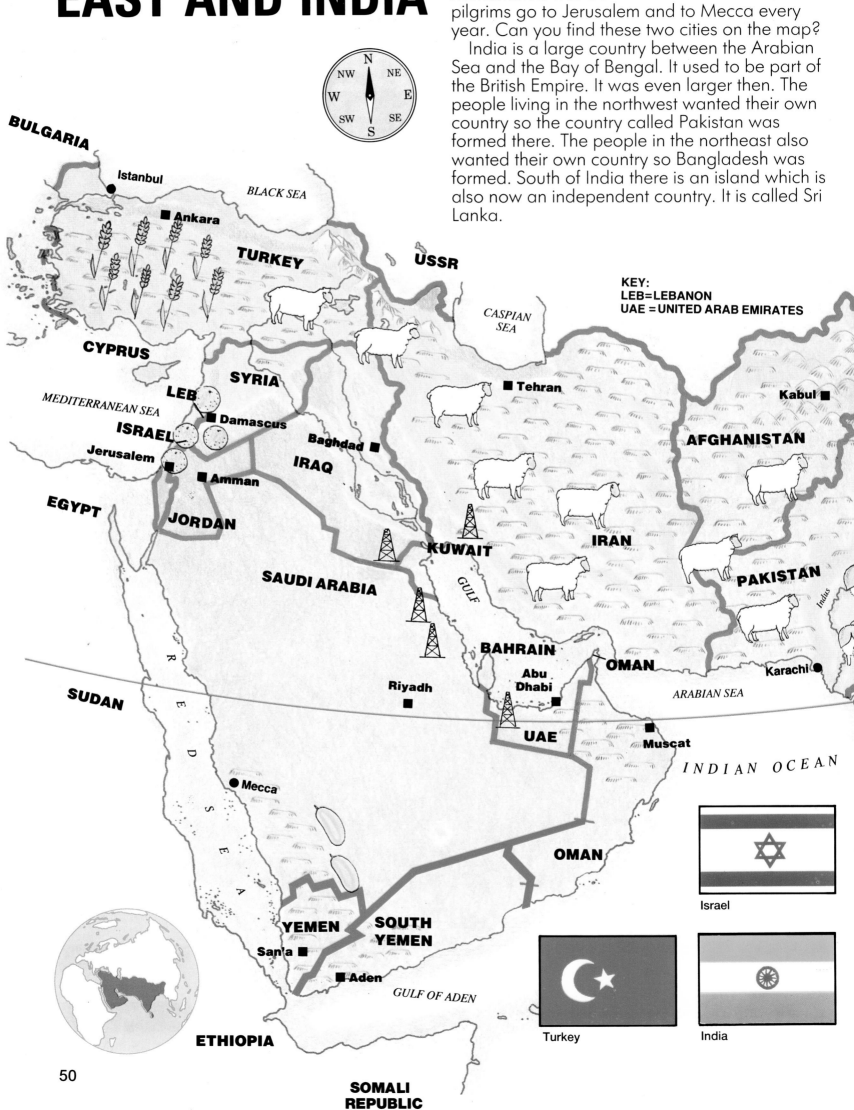

KEY:
LEB=LEBANON
UAE = UNITED ARAB EMIRATES

Israel

Turkey

India

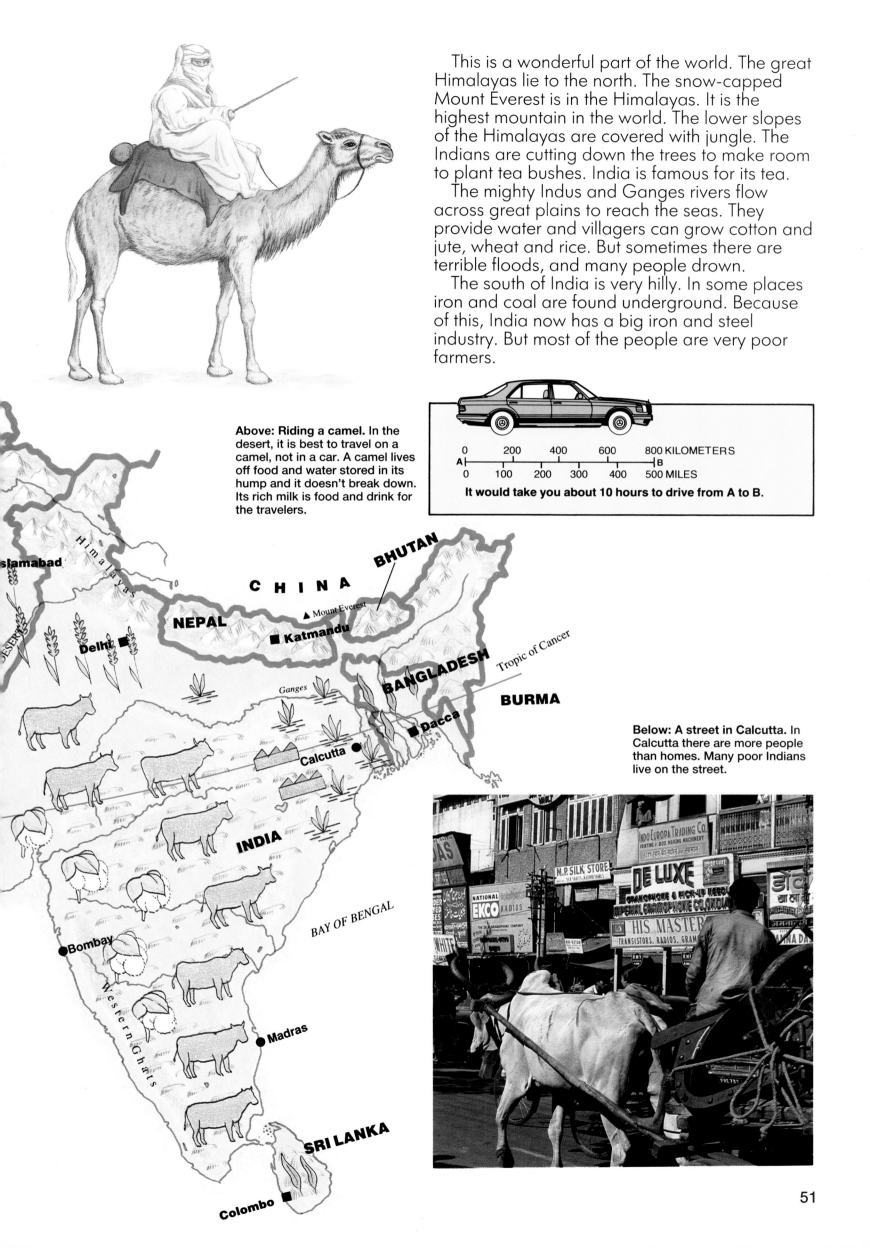

This is a wonderful part of the world. The great Himalayas lie to the north. The snow-capped Mount Everest is in the Himalayas. It is the highest mountain in the world. The lower slopes of the Himalayas are covered with jungle. The Indians are cutting down the trees to make room to plant tea bushes. India is famous for its tea.

The mighty Indus and Ganges rivers flow across great plains to reach the seas. They provide water and villagers can grow cotton and jute, wheat and rice. But sometimes there are terrible floods, and many people drown.

The south of India is very hilly. In some places iron and coal are found underground. Because of this, India now has a big iron and steel industry. But most of the people are very poor farmers.

Above: Riding a camel. In the desert, it is best to travel on a camel, not in a car. A camel lives off food and water stored in its hump and it doesn't break down. Its rich milk is food and drink for the travelers.

0	200	400	600	800 KILOMETERS
0	100 200	300	400	500 MILES

It would take you about 10 hours to drive from A to B.

Below: A street in Calcutta. In Calcutta there are more people than homes. Many poor Indians live on the street.

SOUTHEAST ASIA AND THE EAST INDIES

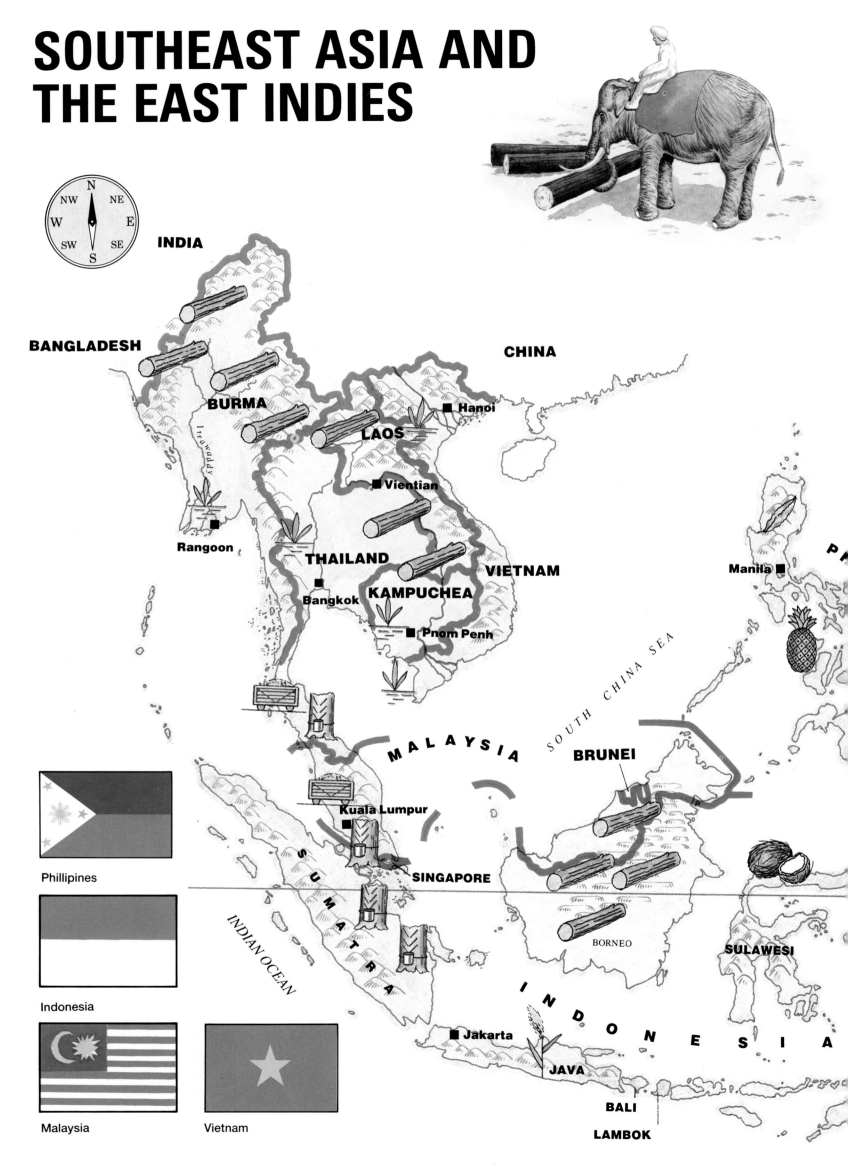

N
NW NE
W E
SW SE
S

INDIA

BANGLADESH

CHINA

BURMA

Irrawaddy

Hanoi

LAOS

Vientian

Rangoon

THAILAND

Bangkok

KAMPUCHEA

Pnom Penh

VIETNAM

Manila

SOUTH CHINA SEA

MALAYSIA

BRUNEI

Kuala Lumpur

SINGAPORE

SUMATRA

INDIAN OCEAN

BORNEO

SULAWESI

INDONESIA

Jakarta

JAVA

BALI

LAMBOK

Phillipines

Indonesia

Malaysia

Vietnam

Left: An elephant. The Indian elephant is easily trained to help us. Elephants are very special animals. The nose has become a trunk. Two of the teeth have become tusks. Tusks are made of ivory and many elephants are killed just to get the ivory.

Right: The Temple of Wat Phrae. The temples and palaces of Thailand are very beautiful. Millions of people go to see them and to pray.

The East Indies is the name we give the islands on the map. Can you see how these islands are in thick and thin lines across the map? This is because there are great mountain ranges under the sea. The islands are just the tips of these mountain ranges.

The Equator runs right across and so it is very hot and wet. The people here used to grow lots of spices such as pepper and cloves and nutmeg. People living in Europe wanted these to use in cooking. Portuguese, Spanish, Dutch, French and English people all sailed to the islands to buy the spices. Then they captured the islands. The Dutch took most, including the large ones such as Sumatra and Java. These do not belong to the Dutch any more but make up the country called Indonesia.

The people still grow spices to sell, but now they also sell rubber from rubber trees, sugar from sugar cane, coconuts from coconut palms and pineapples from the thorny, spiny pineapple plants.

Southeast Asia is made up of Burma, Thailand, Kampuchea, Vietnam, Laos and Western Malaysia. There are great rivers flowing across wide plains. It is so hot and wet that the farmers can grow two crops of rice every year. Between the plains there are great mountain ranges covered with tall trees. Teak trees are sawn down and dragged by elephants to the saw mills. Here they are cut into timber to make expensive furniture.

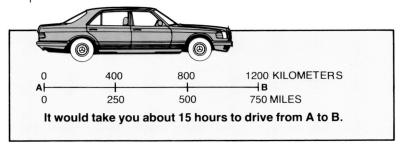

0	400	800	1200 KILOMETERS
A			B
0	250	500	750 MILES

It would take you about 15 hours to drive from A to B.

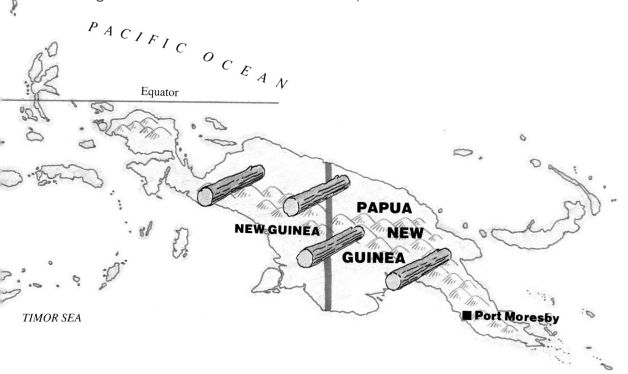

PACIFIC OCEAN

Equator

PAPUA NEW GUINEA

NEW GUINEA

TIMOR SEA

■ Port Moresby

PPINES

CHINA

China is a large country in the continent of Asia. More people live in China than in any other country in the world. There is no language called Chinese; there are very many different languages in China. Chinese people from different towns could not understand each other so they made up a kind of picture-writing so they could write to one another.

The capital city of China is Peking, now called Beijing. The Chinese rulers who lived here were called Mandarins. The language they spoke was called Mandarin. Today, Chinese boys and girls learn to speak Mandarin as well as their own language.

The Chinese are famous for inventing important things such as paper, gunpowder and spectacles.

There are many mountains but also some large fertile plains. In the south, it is hot enough to grow rice, especially in the Red Basin. In the north, they grow wheat, especially on the Great Plain. Chinese teas and silk are famous.

Life is not easy for the Chinese families. There are so many families that each gets only a small share of everything, and so many of them are poor.

The Chinese used to keep themselves to themselves. Now they are letting tourists go into their country. China is changing very fast; it wants to be a modern, industrial country.

Below: The Great Wall of China. The Chinese built the Great Wall to keep out their enemies. Today, tourists walk along it. The Chinese started to build their wall out of stone. Later, they just used earth.

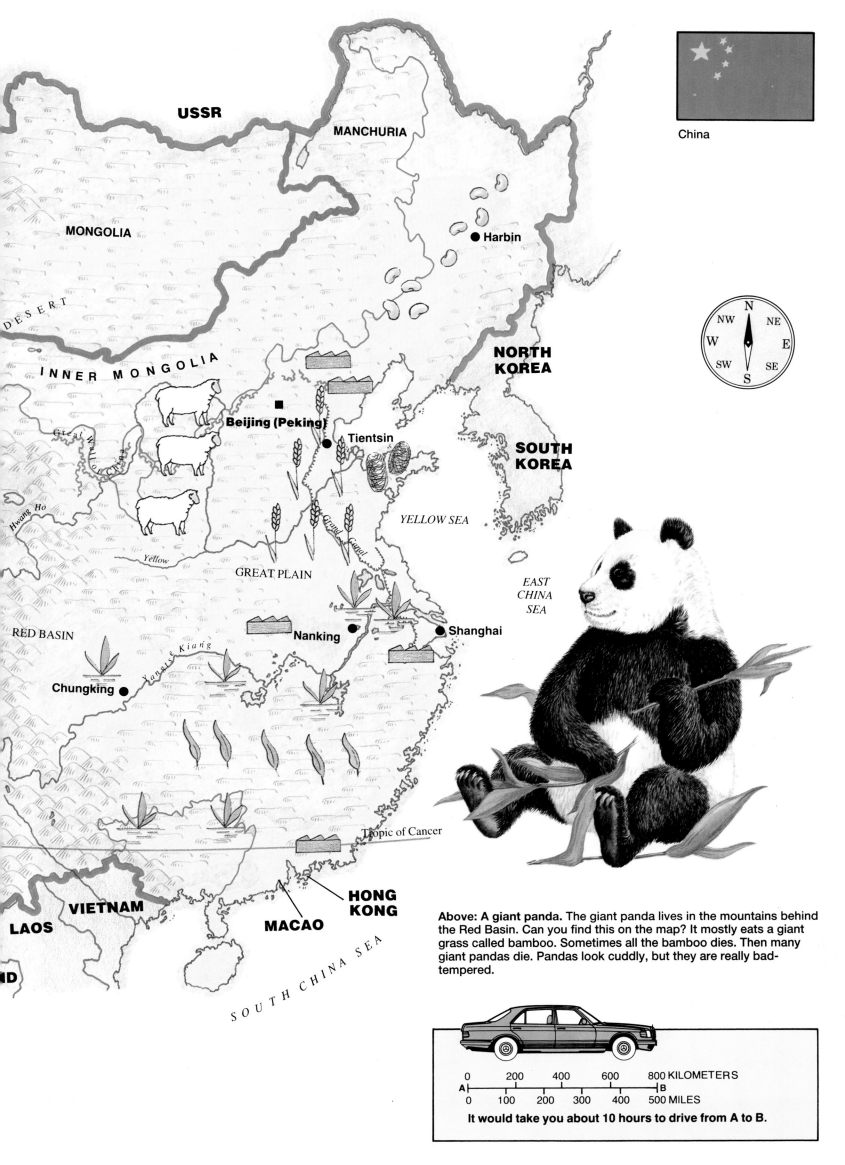

USSR

MANCHURIA

MONGOLIA

● Harbin

DESERT

INNER MONGOLIA

NORTH KOREA

■ Beijing (Peking)

Great Wall of China

● Tientsin

SOUTH KOREA

Hwang Ho

Grand Canal

YELLOW SEA

Yellow

GREAT PLAIN

EAST CHINA SEA

RED BASIN

Yangtse Kiang

Nanking ●

● Shanghai

Chungking ●

Tropic of Cancer

VIETNAM

HONG KONG

LAOS

MACAO

SOUTH CHINA SEA

ND

China

Above: A giant panda. The giant panda lives in the mountains behind the Red Basin. Can you find this on the map? It mostly eats a giant grass called bamboo. Sometimes all the bamboo dies. Then many giant pandas die. Pandas look cuddly, but they are really bad-tempered.

| 0 | 200 | 400 | 600 | 800 KILOMETERS |
| 0 | 100 | 200 | 300 | 400 | 500 MILES |

A   B

It would take you about 10 hours to drive from A to B.

JAPAN, TAIWAN AND KOREA

Japan is a country made up of four large islands and many small ones. The biggest island is called Honshu. Honshu is between the Sea of Japan and the Pacific Ocean. All the islands are very mountainous. Some of the mountains are volcanoes, like the famous Fujiyama. This is an old volcano. It is now quite safe and is so high that there is snow on top. The little islands are really just the tops of mountains sticking up out of the water.

There are a lot of Japanese people, but not enough lowland to grow all the food they need. Therefore they eat lots of fish. They also go all over the world looking for whales to kill and eat, so there are not many whales left any more.

The Japanese make many cars, cameras, computers and robot machines. The Japanese sell them to pay for the extra food they need.

Taiwan is another mountainous island, but it is further south and is therefore hotter. Taiwan is not far from China, and used to belong to China. Everyone works fast and well, and makes lots of clothes, toys and kitchen things to sell abroad.

Above: A Samurai warrior. The Japanese people used to be split into lots of different clans, all fighting one another. Each clan had its own fighters, and they were called Samurai. They were famous for being able to shoot arrows when riding their horses.

Korea used to be one country, but it is now split into two countries. North Korea is next door to the USSR and they help each other. South Korea is all on its own. They built modern schools and factories for themselves, and now they make good cars, ships and clothes to sell to other people.

Below: Mount Fuji.
All the Japanese love Fuji: they paint it, they write poems about it, they climb to the top of it and pray. Where we say mount or mountain, the Japanese say jama or sam, and so an atlas may have the label Fujiyama, Fujisan, Fuji, Mount Fuji or Mount Fujiyama.

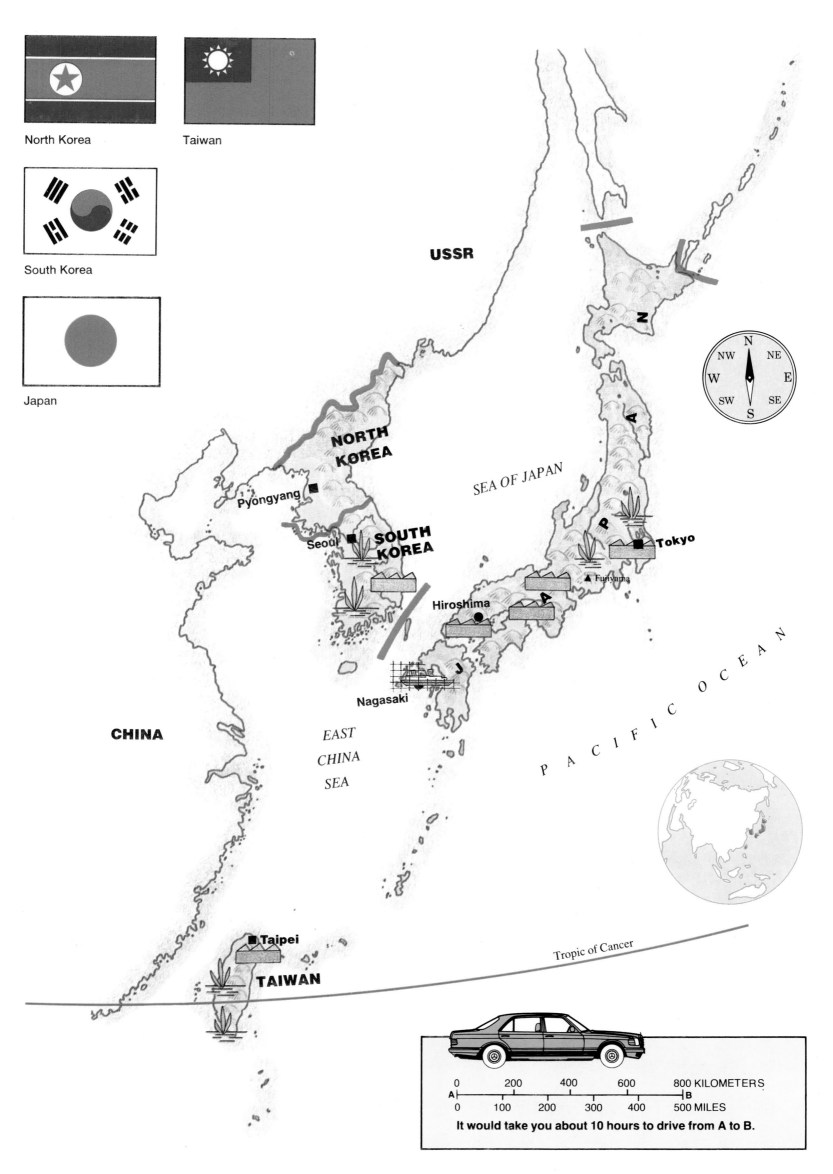

North Korea

Taiwan

South Korea

Japan

USSR

NORTH KOREA

Pyongyang

Seoul

SOUTH KOREA

SEA OF JAPAN

Tokyo

Hiroshima

Fujiyama

Nagasaki

CHINA

EAST CHINA SEA

PACIFIC OCEAN

Taipei

TAIWAN

Tropic of Cancer

NW N NE
W   E
SW S SE

| 0 | 200 | 400 | 600 | 800 KILOMETERS |
| 0 | 100 | 200 | 300 | 400 | 500 MILES |

It would take you about 10 hours to drive from A to B.

AFRICA

The Equator runs right through the middle of Africa. It is always hot and wet here, and there are dense forests. Pygmies live here. Pygmies are a tribe of very small people.

There are more forests in Nigeria and Ghana. The people here grow their food. They also grow cacao trees to get cocoa. They sell this to other countries to make chocolate. And they grow oil palms to get palm oil which is made into soap and margarine.

In the north of Africa is the Sahara Desert. It is full of sand dunes, sheets of pebbles and bare rock. There is no good soil and it is too hot and dry for plants to grow. But there are a few small places with water. These are called oases, and date palms can grow there.

In the south of Africa there is another desert called the Kalahari Desert. A lot of Africa is neither desert nor forest. It is neither very dry nor very wet. It is just right for grasses to grow. Here the Africans grow wheat, maize (corn), cotton and tobacco and they keep cattle for their meat and skins. But some of this part of Africa has not had enough rain for a long time. The crops cannot grow and the people are starving.

Before the Europeans knew about Africa they called it the Dark Continent. Later on they wanted to conquer it. The British took most, but the French, Dutch, Spanish, Portuguese, Italians and Belgians all got some of Africa. They wanted to buy and sell cocoa and palm oil, to mine for gold and diamonds, and to start their own farms. But most of the land has now been given back to the Africans.

MOROCCO

WESTERN SAHARA

MAURITANIA

SENEGAL

GAMBIA

GUINEA BISSAU

GUINEA

SIERRA LEONE

LIBERIA

MALI

UPPER VOLTA

GHANA

IVORY COAST

TO

EQUATORIAL

Below: A street in Cairo. This is the way into the bazaar in Cairo. A bazaar is a kind of open-air market. There are stalls instead of shops. You can easily get lost in a big bazaar!

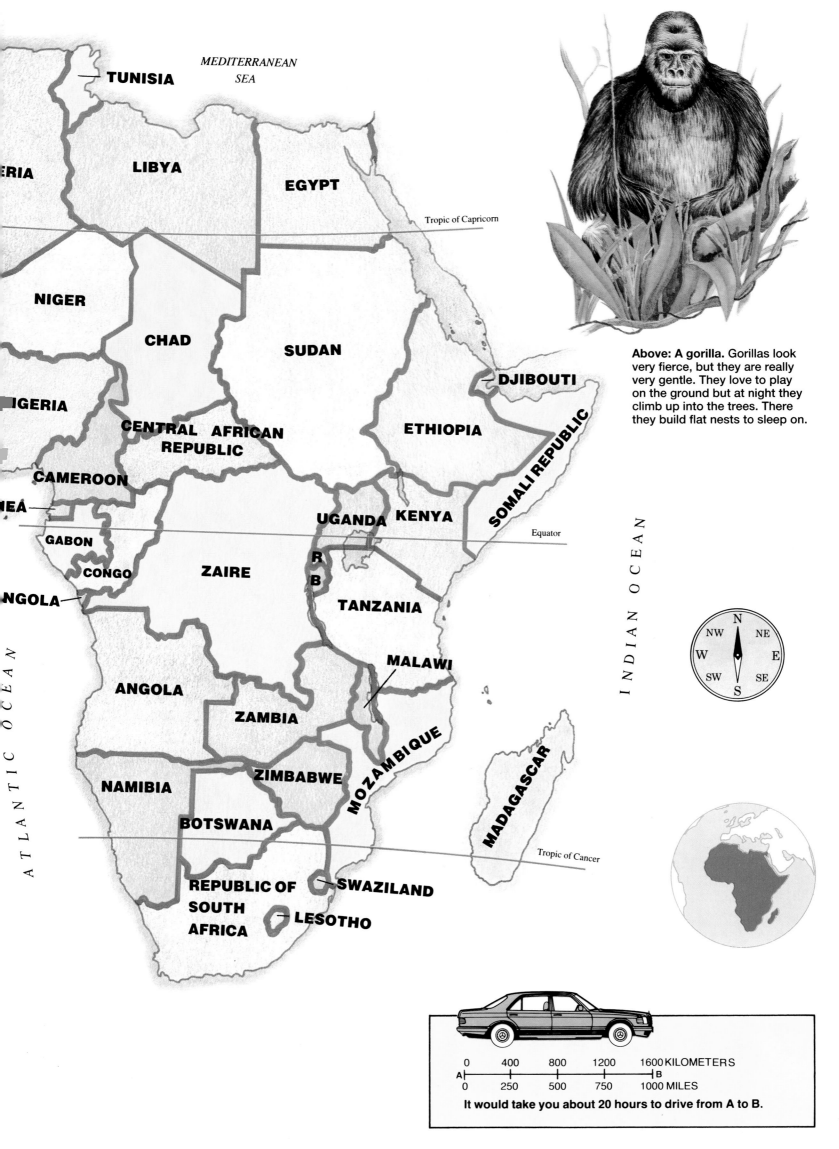

KEY
B = BURUNDI
R = RWANDA

MEDITERRANEAN SEA

TUNISIA

LIBYA

EGYPT

Tropic of Capricorn

NIGER

CHAD

SUDAN

DJIBOUTI

IGERIA

CENTRAL AFRICAN REPUBLIC

ETHIOPIA

CAMEROON

NEA

UGANDA   KENYA

SOMALI REPUBLIC

GABON

Equator

CONGO

ZAIRE

R
B

NGOLA

TANZANIA

INDIAN OCEAN

MALAWI

ATLANTIC OCEAN

ANGOLA

ZAMBIA

MOZAMBIQUE

MADAGASCAR

Tropic of Cancer

NAMIBIA

ZIMBABWE

BOTSWANA

REPUBLIC OF SOUTH AFRICA

SWAZILAND

LESOTHO

Above: A gorilla. Gorillas look very fierce, but they are really very gentle. They love to play on the ground but at night they climb up into the trees. There they build flat nests to sleep on.

N
NW   NE
W   E
SW   SE
S

0   400   800   1200   1600 KILOMETERS
A|------|------|------|------|B
0   250   500   750   1000 MILES
It would take you about 20 hours to drive from A to B.

59

NORTHERN AFRICA

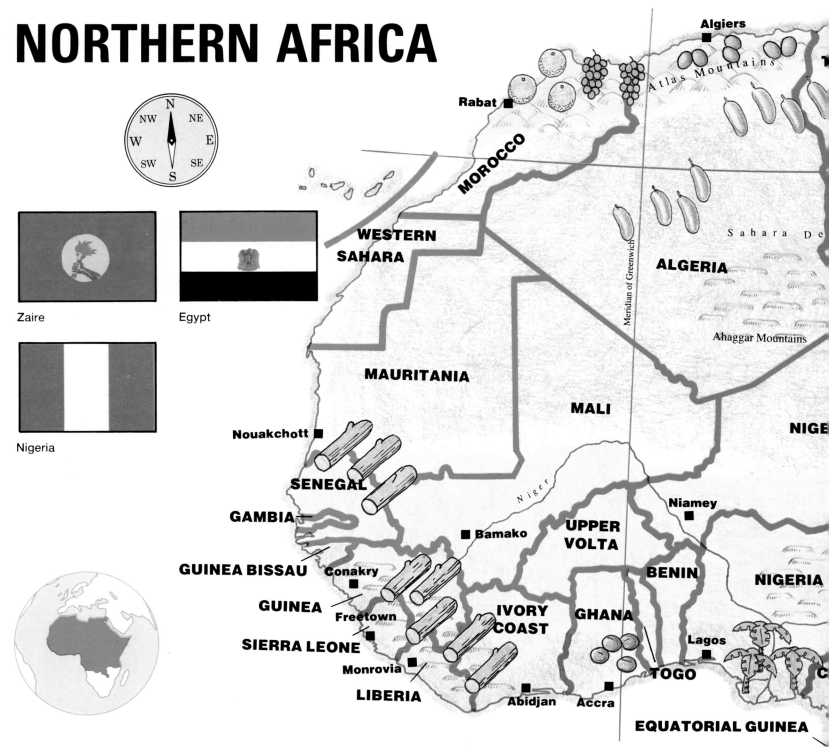

Zaire

Egypt

Nigeria

The great river Nile begins in the mountains of the south. It then flows northwards across the Sahara Desert, all the way to the Mediterranean Sea. The Nile brings water to the desert.

This was one of the first places in the world where the people stopped hunting for food and began to grow it instead. They grew wheat and barley, onions and beans. Every year the great Nile flooded the fields on either side before rushing down to the sea. The people planted seeds in the rich, wet, warm mud.

These people were the Egyptians and their kings were called pharaohs. Egypt became a very rich country. Vast palaces and temples were built, and the pharaohs were buried inside great pyramids and tombs.

The modern Egyptians do not wait for the yearly floods. They have built a great dam across the Nile called the Aswan Dam. This holds all the flood water, so it can be used all year round.

Morocco, Algeria and Tunisia take up northwest Africa. It often rains here. Because of this, the farmers can grow many things, including almonds, grapes and oranges.

All over the Sahara Desert one can find pots full of dried-up food buried in the sand. Tools used by farmers and their wives long ago have also been found. These must have been used before the Sahara was a desert. We are not sure why the Sahara became a desert. Some scientists think that it simply stopped raining there. Others believe that the wind blew away all the good soil, leaving only poor sand.

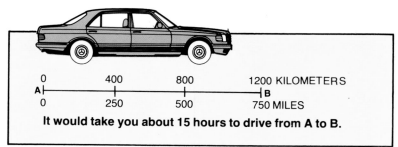

It would take you about 15 hours to drive from A to B.

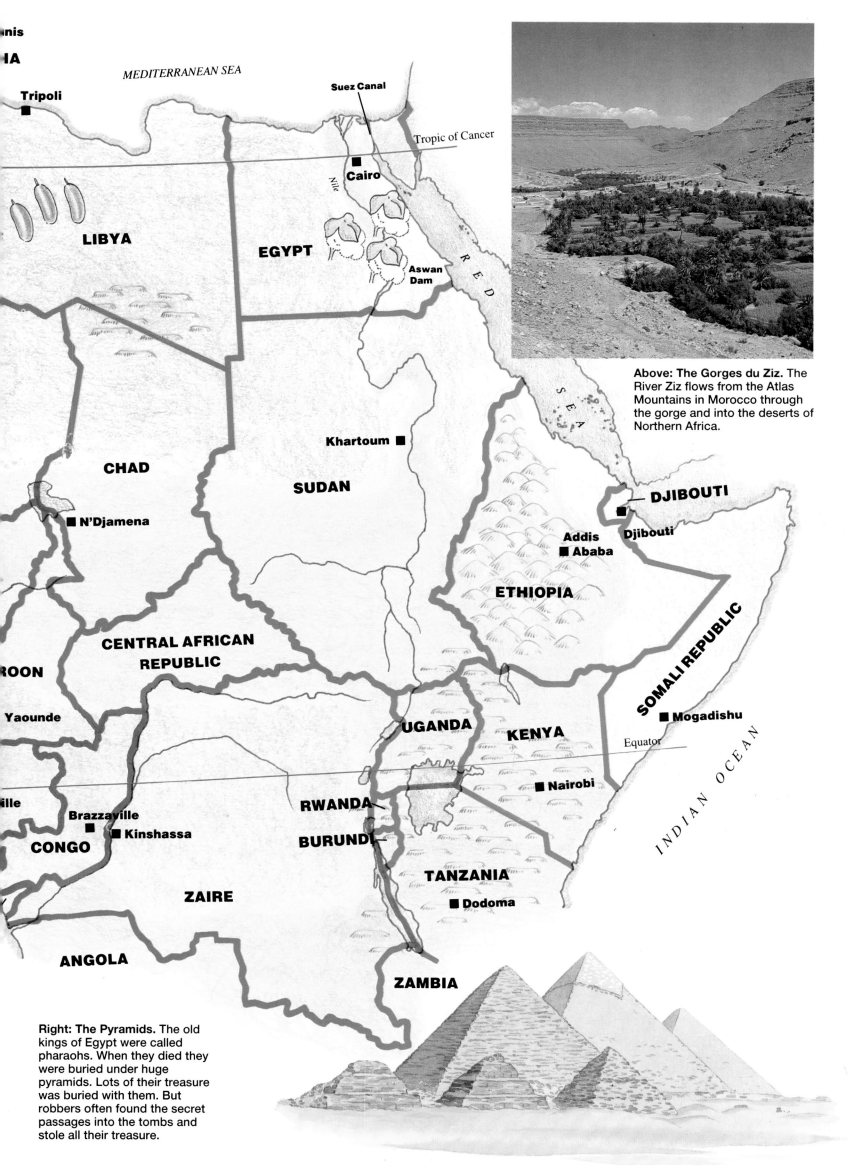

MEDITERRANEAN SEA

Tripoli ■

Suez Canal

Tropic of Cancer

Nile

Cairo ■

LIBYA

EGYPT

Aswan Dam

RED

nis

HA

Above: The Gorges du Ziz. The River Ziz flows from the Atlas Mountains in Morocco through the gorge and into the deserts of Northern Africa.

SEA

CHAD

SUDAN

Khartoum ■

■ N'Djamena

DJIBOUTI

Addis
Ababa ■

Djibouti

CENTRAL AFRICAN
REPUBLIC

ETHIOPIA

SOMALI REPUBLIC

ROON

Yaounde

UGANDA

KENYA

Equator

■ Mogadishu

ille

Brazzaville

■ Kinshassa

RWANDA

BURUNDI

■ Nairobi

CONGO

TANZANIA

INDIAN OCEAN

ZAIRE

■ Dodoma

ANGOLA

ZAMBIA

Right: The Pyramids. The old kings of Egypt were called pharaohs. When they died they were buried under huge pyramids. Lots of their treasure was buried with them. But robbers often found the secret passages into the tombs and stole all their treasure.

SOUTHERN AFRICA

A long time ago, all this part of Africa used to belong to Bushmen and Hottentots. Most of it is a flat grassy plateau. People called Zulus wanted the land for their cattle, and year by year they moved in. The peaceful Bushmen and Hottentots were driven out to live in the Kalahari Desert.

Dutch and English farmers then wanted to come to the rich grasslands. They fought the Zulus to see who would win the land. After many battles, the Europeans won. Then they found the biggest ever goldfield at Johannesburg and the largest diamonds ever at Kimberley. Much of the land, like the countries Zambia and Zimbabwe, has now been given back to the Africans.

Most people in Southern Africa are farmers. Some countries have minerals which they sell to other countries around the world. Antelopes, giraffes, gnus, zebras, rhinoceroses and elephants — and lions which prey on them — still feed on the grassy plateau.

Above: Safari in Southern Africa. These elephants are being watched by tourists. Each year, hundreds of tourists go on safari through the African game reserves in order to see the animals in their natural environment.

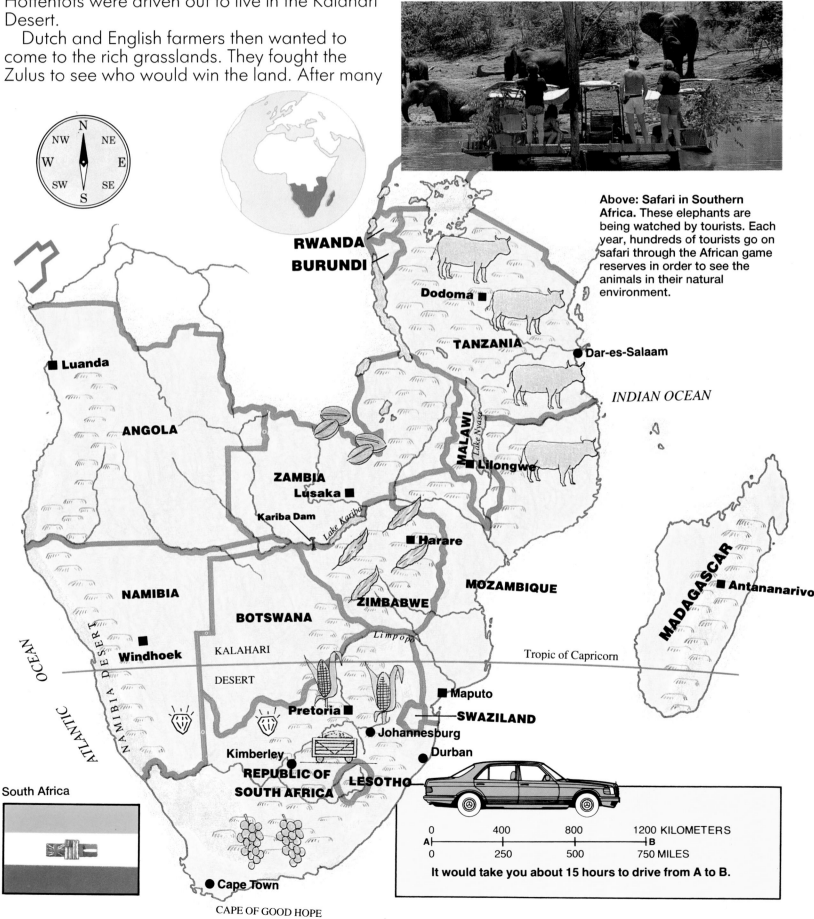

South Africa

It would take you about 15 hours to drive from A to B.

THE COMPASS

Compass points. A compass tells you which direction is North, South, East and West. Some of the points in between are Northeast, Northwest, Southeast, Southwest (NE, NW, SE, SW). There is a compass like this on every map.

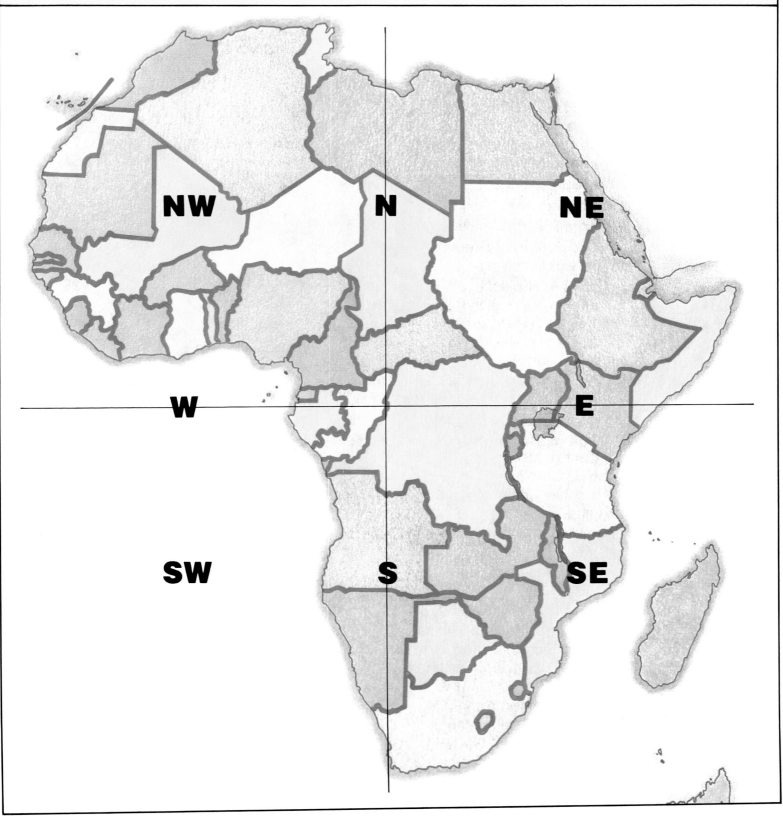